WOMEN
RISING

CHANTELLE ADAMS
&
17 COURAGEOUS WOMEN

WOMEN RISING Volume III

Copyright © 2017 Chantelle Adams – Chantelle Adams Enterprises Inc.
www.chantelleadams.com

Editor: Beth Jarrell

Published by STOKE Publishing
www.stokepublishing.com

ISBN: 978-1-988675-04-6
Self-Help/Women's Studies

Dedication

This book is dedicated to all the women in the world who do not feel they have a voice.
Who feel their story doesn't matter. It does.
Now is the time for women everywhere to rise up and share their messages of hope, tragedy, and strength.

Rise UP.
Speak your truth.
Lend your voice.
Share your wisdom.

It is time to...
Get real.
Become vulnerable.
Be seen.

This book is for every woman who longs to be heard, who is struggling, who has been lost and who is in the midst of the storm.

There is hope.
There is freedom.
There is strength.
You can find it within.

It is time to write your story,
decide your fate and create the life you desire.
Our stories are the gateway to our souls; they unlock the keys to our future and become the catalyst for change in our lives and the world.

Let us rise together.

Table of Contents

Introduction

This is a compilation of women's voices sharing their stories of heartache, loss, struggle and the beautiful lessons they learned while going through these difficult moments in their lives.

Their stories may echo yours. You will feel their pain, embrace their heart and together, learn the lessons they learned in their own paths of discovery.

In your life, there are times when it feels like your whole world has been turned upside down. When you hit a wall and feel like everything has fallen apart and then something changes within you, everything shifts.

This is your breakdown moment, the moment where you realize that something has to change and that you have the power within you to make it happen.

Every breakdown has the potential to lead into a breakthrough if you are open to digging deep and looking within for guidance and truth.

This is the moment when everything changes and you begin to make the climb upwards. You find a renewed sense of hope and little by little you learn along the way the lessons these struggles have taught you.

You see how it has made you stronger.

You have become more aware of the power you have to choose. You see that every day is a new day and a new opportunity to be seized.

You discover the beauty that is around you.

You learn to embrace the moment, forgive those who have hurt you, trust in your own guiding power and act with courage.

These women have overcome the odds, have fought a great fight, have lost and loved, have come to the moment that could break them and chosen to walk a new path and light their own way.

You will find every story unique, powerful and full of lessons that have the power to change your life.

This is a book that will renew your faith in the ability to truly live when all feels lost.

The Dalai Lama once said so eloquently, *"The world will be saved by the western woman."*

It is time to rise up.

Read on, and join us in speaking your truth, sharing your story and changing the world together, one voice at a time.

Chantelle Adams | www.chantelleadams.com

Chapter 1

So. About That Affair.
When shame translates into self-destruction, the only way out is through connection and self-compassion.

"Women need a tribe to lead the world." - Dimple Mukherjee

I remember the feeling of lightness. This feeling can be best described as floating amongst fluffy, white, angelic clouds without any heaviness to pull you down. Perhaps that's what freedom feels like? I knew that feeling of lightness as a child, but then a force greater than myself decided I had it too good and the light started to dim, slowly but surely until there was nothing but stark darkness.

My life had been a sheltered one. Born in India and raised in Taiwan under some strict rules set by traditional Indian parents, I lived in a bubble and was clueless about reality. I wasn't a rebel. I followed rules. I played it safe. I was comfortable with others making decisions for me, which I came to learn was more dangerous than making the wrong choices for myself. But surprisingly, with all those rules also came optimism. I didn't need to know what was going on outside, because I was so cared for on the inside. Privileged, protected and painfully inexperienced. Weaving in and out of life being the eternal optimist was effortless for me until I started second-guessing my life after marriage.

I married young. I was only 23-years-old. I had my first child at the age of 25. I was socially conditioned to believe that this was the way you "should" live your life and find happiness. Combine all these things with a lack of life experiences and, well, you can only imagine my predicament. Rules dictated my life so much that I didn't have to really think about planning my life out - it was all planned for me already. My old self would say that life was decent... and then I hit 30.

I'm embarrassed to admit, but my 30's were an epic fail. My marriage was in the pits, but I refused to admit it because doing so would mean opening myself up to the naysayers, cultural bigots and judgmental onlookers. I was knee-deep in shame. Shame prevented me from reaching for that one thing I needed the most- connection. I chose self-destruction instead.

To say that I lost myself entirely in pain numbing behaviours would be an understatement. Partying, drinking, flirting, shopping- anything comforting to distract me from my life, and it was dangerous. I couldn't wait for nightfall because it meant I could retreat into my sacred haven, my bedroom, and shove all my worries away under my massive, king sized, organic cotton pillow. Sleep was therapeutic, but also numbing for me.

Worst of all, I had these three lil' boys. They were longing for my attention, but I had very little to give back to them. Even in a house full of toys, football plays, belly laughs, silly jokes and constant sibling shenanigans, I felt alone and empty. A toxic energy lingered. I felt it in my gut. Negativity, heaviness and dirty laundry. I clung on to my daily morning rituals of meditation, greens, lemon water, coffee, dancing and journaling for dear life. If not for these life saving practices, the little bit of sanity I had left would have escaped me. I continued to struggle with feelings of unease, isolation, restlessness, fear and anger.

I knew my big, bad secret was brewing and bubbling, waiting to explode and blow my life wide open. I knew it would happen any day now.

Loud, blaring music from a wedding procession was echoing in my hotel room from the balcony as I strained to listen to the desperate voice of my then husband who was calling me long-distance from Toronto. Breathing became so laborious that it actually hurt. I was all dolled up in my black and gold sari and just two minutes earlier, was as excited as I could be to step outside and join the rest of the colorful clan of family members in the sweltering heat for wedding festivities. My oldest nephew was getting married in India and I couldn't wait to dance up a storm. That was before my entire world came crashing down.

Life was never the same after that call. My husband had found out about my affair. I had some serious decisions to make and none that were clear even though you might think they were. If I stayed to restore it all, to heal, to take away his pain, I knew nothing would change and I would be back to my old patterns or worse, he would. In the moment of crisis, it felt natural to desire comfort, familiarity and most of all, to numb the pain. But unfortunately, that system was broken and didn't work.

I decided that my marriage had to end. In that moment, I knew this was my chance to lead a better life. Too much was damaged beyond repair and while this decision was incredibly painful, it was the right thing to do. Even if our marriage had the slightest chance of reconciliation, it would require years and years of healing and self-growth – but on our own and not together. That was the brutal truth. It took three years for both of us to accept that.

Slowly but surely, my husband and I took the baby steps we needed to detach, but I can assure you that road was topsy-turvy at best. I thought the hardest part was over. My next move now would be to just handle the logistics regarding the divorce, ensure that my children were well-adjusted to all the changes and finally build a respectful relationship with the current man in my life.

With this newfound freedom I lost my way yet again, like a little girl in a store full of bubblegum and candies, all the bad disguised in irresistible packaging. As my marriage ended, so did my need to hide. Life was starting to feel a bit sparkly again. It was my chance to start over and create a new beginning. I felt it was owed to me. The shame that I experienced had been debilitating and here was an opportunity to earn back my respect with all my might.

The good news is that as I set about on this mission, I blossomed. My new life emerged and it didn't go the slightest bit unnoticed. I felt I belonged and accepted as I started to share bits and pieces of my story with other women. My journey towards a path of service and meaning was beckoning. I was as hungry for it as it was for me.

The bad news was that without the protective shell of secrecy, I couldn't fake a happy ending to my fairytale romance. The affair became an expired relationship. The crazy thing about evolution is that you inevitably leave behind those who don't grow alongside with you, and that is exactly what happened in my story. More pain engulfed me and a million and one 'whys' circled around in my head. And then one day, I got it.

Let me remind you that by this point in time, I had taken a gazillion self help courses, read a ton of books, and followed mentors around ad nauseam. So while it would seem this realization came to me seamlessly, I can assure you it didn't. I was carrying around a burden so heavy that I couldn't see past its ironclad façade.

I wasn't good enough.

I took the plunge and left him too. It was a bittersweet ending to what I had imagined to be so much more than it actually was. Talk about the ultimate shame. All I had to show for now was two failed relationships, yet I took that bold step and I can't believe I did. But before I did, I gathered my troop-my friends, my counselor, my mentors and most of all, my women, my tribe. I finally allowed myself permission to seek them out and more importantly, ask for compassion so that I could let go the last of my blockages and in return, extend that compassion to myself for the ultimate growth.

I found my liberation when I was finally able to convince myself that I was worthy of something better – much better. It took me 40 years of my life to arrive at this simple, most beautiful truth. In the midst of all this messiness, I trusted the process but was terrified of the pain. When I accepted that pain too has a real purpose as part of my existence, I embraced it wholeheartedly and no longer numbed it. As soon as I mustered up the courage to sit in this pain, I was much further ahead, much faster. I didn't do it alone. I did it in the company of powerful women who allowed themselves to be vulnerable just as I eventually did.

I grew exponentially that year. I travelled to exotic cities. My ex-husband and I actually became friends and hung out! (That was a biggie). Our children benefited immensely from this positive energy and are amazing resilient beings. I formed Bindi Parlour, a sacred space for women to just be. Best of all, I found self love leads to real love.

Today I live my life from a place of self-compassion and am passionate about female connections as my number one "go to" tool for expansion. But first, I always start with me- my core and my truth- just as I did when I was in the midst of chaos. White space for clarity was my lifeline. There is no way around this work. If I wanted to create a lifetime of happiness for myself, my family and ultimately those around me, I had to bring in the energy I wanted to see in this world. I became conscious about my tendencies for pain-numbing behaviours and replaced them with soul-soothing practices that continuously elevate my life and nourish me, so that I can spread my wings even further.

As I cultivated a transformative and healing lifestyle, I was mindful of the fact that those who inspired me the most to take courageous acts towards the life of my dreams were everyday women. Women who had mastered the art of connection through their stories and weren't afraid of showing up fully to change the world. In this safe space, even as an observer, I felt invincible and confident. If she can do it then so can I. Harnessing this powerful energy was a key step in both building momentum & motivation and for taking that next big, scary step.

Ultimately, in this stability and security where I fully controlled the reigns, owned my story and co-created my reality, I was able to not only receive and release in the comfort of other women, but also give back. Once I knew who my women were, I started gathering, in person and online. I witnessed tears, laughter, honesty and full-on trust. The deep level of trust was really what blew my mind and therein was the foundation for the safety that we all crave so that we can hold space for each other. It's that simple. It's that pure. Anything and everything is possible from that space.

As I stack my life lessons, one on top of another, I am reminded ever so subtly that this is how beliefs are formed. Allow me to share my latest core belief and one that has never steered me wrong:

Women need a tribe to lead the world.

If you continue to hold yourself back from living a life of freedom because of shame & fear of vulnerability and succumb to pain-numbing behaviours, then you could very well end up as I did. But, I am willing to bet that if you knew there were other women just like you who have your back, you wouldn't play small.

What would you do differently if you knew there was a tribe of women behind you, cheering you on every step of the way?

Let's make it happen! Here's how to gather your women so that you can elevate your life:

First, get to know yourself really well so that you can invite the right kind of female connections into your life. Dedicate at least 10 minutes or more to daily practices that feed your soul. Movement, journaling, singing, meditating- whatever ignites your spark.

Second, seek out and follow online female mentors. Make them your daily dose of inspiration to help you stay committed to your vision.

Third, be an active participant in women's circles, groups, retreats, conferences and events to grow your tribe. My tribe today came about as a result of amazing connections that were created in such gatherings.

Start Now. Your tribe is waiting!

Meet Dimple

Dimple Mukherjee is a Women's Coach who combines 20-plus years of experience as an Occupational Therapist with Integrative Health Coaching and Positive Psychology certifications to help women harness the healing and transformative power of female connections for personal growth. Dimple created Bindi Parlour, a safe space for women to embrace themselves and to create positive shifts in their lives through conversations and soul play. The truth is, women need a tribe to lead the world.

After a career in occupational therapy, three children, some rock-bottom moments and a second career, Dimple ultimately came to the realization that she lost some of the best years of her life to shame. Shame is debilitating, self-destructive and will stop women from shining. Today, Dimple is passionate about sharing her personal stories to teach women how to break free from the reigns of shame through self-compassion, empathy and connection. As Brené Brown, shame researcher, says, *"Shame needs secrecy, silence and judgment to grow but shame cannot survive empathy."* What Dimple knows for sure is that when women gather, create safety, and share vulnerable stories, shame ceases to exist. Her wish is for every woman to step into her light from this space so that she can be the change maker that our world desperately needs.

When she is not helping women ignite their inner spark, Dimple loves to travel all over the world, dance to Bollywood music, is on a constant path of self learning (think tons and tons of books and courses), volunteers her time with Everyday Child, parents teenagers (a full-time gig and then some) and is busy dreaming up a way of purchasing that beach home in the Caribbean.

If you are ready to connect with your tribe to lead the world, join us here. We saved you a seat.

www.dimplemukherjee.com

Chapter 2

Maxed Out Mom Turns Millennial
How to lead your life and love the journey

"Everything you want is on the other side of deciding it is possible!" – Mary Ottman

Are you a wife or mom balancing work with raising a family? Do you have someone in your life that depends on you, perhaps, for example, an elderly parent? Are you a boss or employee working your tail off with no life-work balance?

On top of that long list, do you also manage to fit in trips to the grocery store, cook meals and provide Mom's Taxi Service to your kids? Do your kids have a better social life than you do? Do you put your own needs last on your list because you have mom-guilt for not spending as much time as you think you should with your family?

All of that adds up to a ton of long days, not getting enough sleep and constant stress. I have been where you are and I totally get it; all of the roles you play are important to you. However, there is a problem with this scenario.

Did you know that, according to the Centers for Disease Control and Prevention, heart disease is the leading cause of death for women in the United States, resulting in one out every four female deaths? Furthermore, doctors have determined that stress is a significant contributor to heart disease. These statistics highlight that our current cultural expectation of cramming every aspect of our lives with stressful busyness is not good for our health. In fact, these statistics indicate that we could LITERALLY work ourselves into an early grave by subjecting ourselves to constant stress.

When I leaned over the counter of my doctor's office to read the results of my MRI brain scan, my heart just stopped. I was absolutely stunned. I remember feeling a huge lump in my throat and I read the results again and again. The doctor had asked his assistant to pull up the results while he stepped out, and then she too stepped out while I read them. There I was, totally alone, reading that I had tiny scars on my brain that could be caused by either Multiple Sclerosis or migraines. Multiple Sclerosis. Wow.

That moment was my own worst fear coming to life. I stood there in the doctor's office envisioning myself encased in a body that could not function on its own while my active brain lay trapped inside. This could not be happening to me. I was the girl who jumped off the roof of the 108-story Stratosphere Hotel in Vegas. I was the world traveler, always hopping on an airplane heading to another exotic locale. As I stood there, it was as if my brain just stopped processing any of this. At the same time, my mind was racing with all the different reasons this could not be happening to me.

When you become a mom, you never envision that you will die before your child has grown up and has a family of her own. You never picture a future where you are not there for her college graduation or helping her plan all the joyous details for her wedding. You cannot imagine not being there to support her when your little grandbabies come into the world.

As I stood there, stunned, all these thoughts going through my head, the doctor reappeared. He tried to give me comforting advice, but I barely heard him since I was still in shock. He said that the MRI results were inconclusive and that if it was MS, he knew people that had been treated into remission. That was very good to know, and yet it did not stop me from envisioning the possible worst-case scenarios.

I spent several days going over the diagnosis again and again in my head, crying my eyes out every night. I remember sitting in the dark in my little apartment living room. I envisioned my daughter alone in the world without her Mama. Who would she go to when she was anxious and overwhelmed? Who would tease her out of her need to overanalyze and account for every possible horrible contingency she could envision? Who would comfort her and convince her that her problems were not as big as she thought?

One night, sitting in my favorite chair in my living room, I decided that I would write a book and dedicate it to my daughter. This book would contain all the life lessons that I wanted to pass along to her in case I was not there to love her as only her Mama can. I knew that in order to write this book, I needed to change my lifestyle, because I was not taking care of myself and I needed to be her role model.

My daughter grew up seeing me work really hard. I worked long hours and traveled extensively for business. I remember one year for Mother's Day she gave me lavender stress relief lotion. That should have been a clue I worked too much, right? She also brought home a hand-made Mother's Day card from school. They had asked her to fill-in-the-blank on several questions like "What does your mother do?" Thinking back, and my memory is not what it used to be, all her answers indicated her mom worked all the time. I remember it hurt my heart to read that, but being divorced at the time, I thought I really did not have a choice.

So there I was, a few years later with my scarred brain, my heart palpitations, dizzy spells, stomach problems and migraines, and I knew it was time to make a big change. I began my quest for knowledge on how to handle work-life balance, and I came across several articles referring to millennials that were extremely interesting. I read these articles and their associated commentary on how to deal with millennials at the workplace. There were articles that stated millennials were self-entitled and sitting around waiting for a career to be handed to them. I knew that was not the case with my own homegrown millennial- my daughter - and I decided to dig a little deeper.

I did some research, read articles and social media posts written by millennials, then went out and talked with them about these millennial stereotypes. As it turns out, I learned three pretty amazing things.

1) Many millennials were very interested in planning their long-term career from the time they joined the professional workforce

I have seen older generations attribute this to self-entitlement. I have seen and heard older workforce members become seriously annoyed by this millennial tendency to do early career planning. When the young whippersnappers walked in the door on their first day asking how to get a promotion, I heard comments like, "They just need to do what I did and work for a while and be happy they have a job, then worry about getting a promotion."

But here is the thing: what is wrong with this millennial approach to career planning? I'll tell you what is wrong with it….ABSOLUTELY NOTHING! Heck, I wish I had started that early in my own career. Just think how much further we would have gotten in our careers if we started on day one accepting every opportunity that came our way when it met our long-term career aspirations. We would have maximized our time, gotten promotions sooner and started making more money much earlier in our careers.

Making more money sooner in one's career can contribute to better relationships at home, since finances tend to be one of the largest trouble areas in marriages. In addition, making more money sooner can lead to being able to afford more vacations, which can lead to reducing stress as well.

I don't know about you, but this Maxed-Out Mom is ready to turn millennial right now. I think they are onto something with this approach.

2) Millennials want their work to matter and they want to make a difference in the world

Many millennials are service-oriented. They want to change lives and make meaningful contributions. However, the attitude at the typical workplace goes something like this: "We hired you to do this job, so can you do the job you were assigned? We don't change lives here. We just need you to get this done by Friday."

I have to say, I am in the millennial camp on this. I am in my 40's now, and I try every single day to do work that matters. I do not want to work where I do not make a difference.

Since I agree with the millennial perspective, I have to ask, what is wrong with wanting to help people? I'll tell you what is wrong with it... ABSOLUTELY NOTHING! Imagine what our communities would look like now if we had started focusing on making a difference twenty years earlier in our lives. In addition, finding a purpose and volunteering to serve others can serve as a stress-reliever and a mood-lifting activity as well.

3) Millennials want work-life balance. They're smart cookies. Many of them grew up as latchkey kids, entertaining themselves until we made it home through rush hour traffic. They have seen us work really long hours and miss their baseball games or their dance recitals, and those were a big deal for these guys when they were little. Millennials have experienced all this and they do not want to work 60 – 70 hour weeks and miss out on having a life.

Although some long-term employees inundate the millennials with the, "That's the way it's always been done" mentality, kudos to these guys and gals for challenging the status quo of our frenetic culture! The great news is that the medical community agrees with them in that work-life balance is important for reducing stress and maximizing good health.

After reading and hearing the hype in the press and in the workplace, it is my view that millennials are getting a bad rap. These kids are savvy and they push the boundaries on existing ways of thinking. With the #1 cause of death in women being heart disease and stress being a significant contributing factor, we definitely need to find new ways to incorporate stress reduction and balance into our hectic lives. I would suggest that we look at adopting the millennial perspective on this balance as soon as possible! We cannot go back and change our past, but we can start today to make positive changes. By planning our careers from this point forward, we can be better equipped for challenges like layoffs and financial emergencies thanks in part to getting promotions and making more money sooner in our careers. Secondly, helping others is a great way to reduce stress and take our minds off our own troubles. Finally, by pursuing work-life balance, we can spend more time with our family and friends. By having less stress and more free time, we tend to be more emotionally and physically present for our family and friends so we have better relationships. All three of these millennial behaviors lead to less stress, better work-life balance and better overall health. After considering all the benefits, this Maxed-Out Mom is ready to put her millennial game face on!

Rise Up Challenge

I would love to raise a toast to all you moms, wives, lady bosses and employees everywhere. You gorgeous girls do not get nearly enough kudos for taking such great care of your families while working hard to make a difference in the lives of others. I am so inspired by all of you!

With that being said, I know that there is so much more inside of you just dying to come out and make a life-changing contribution to the world. I want to challenge each of you to show up in the world as even more of your big, bold and authentic self by embracing the millennials' approach to living life with balance.

Here are three ways you can take millennial-inspired action to lead your life and love the journey starting today:

- Your first challenge involves millennial-like career planning, starting today! Book a couple of hours on your calendar just for you to think about your aspirations, what is not working in your life, and which areas you are ready to take action and change. Where do you want to be in 5, 10 and 15 years from now? I know this will be extremely difficult for some of you, but YOU deserve the best future for YOU!

- Your second challenge gets you out of the house and making a difference in your community, millennial style! Everybody has a cause that is near and dear to their heart. It is the one that causes you deep sadness when you think about the need in that area.

  Are you an ardent pet lover who is touched deeply at the sight of abused and neglected animals? Do you have a fondness for the elderly who could benefit from your care and your time if you regularly visited a retirement home? Are you deeply moved by causes that help combat hunger and poverty in your community?

Your challenge is to pick one cause that thrills you to be part of and set up a meeting to talk with them and sign up to be a volunteer. This can truly be a life-changing effort, for both you and the people you will serve!

- Your third and final challenge is to create millennial-inspired boundaries around your work-life balance. Get out of the house and get a life! You deserve a wonderful life brimming with time for yourself. Set up boundaries such as not checking work emails after 9 p.m. Schedule a weekly massage to help with stress relief. Schedule a monthly Girl's Night Out with ladies who inspire you. If you know a millennial, take them out to lunch. Millennials are raising awareness that work-life balance is necessary and they are right. It is time we Maxed-Out Moms turn millennial and start enjoying our lives to the fullest!

And the Multiple Sclerosis? I never took the test to determine whether or not I have MS. I do have migraines, so I believe my scarred brain is due to the headaches. In case you think I am in denial, let me just confirm that for you- I am 100% in denial. Whether I do or do not have MS, I vow to enjoy my life to the absolute fullest with an optimal work-life balance while I pursue my mission of empowering women to be leaders.

Speaking of empowering women, I sincerely hope my daughter embraces the importance of leading her life with work-life balance so that she can love her own journey. If she powerfully shines her amazing, beautiful, talented light in this world, I can rest easy knowing that I have done my job as her mother. Kayla, I am so very proud of you. I am truly the luckiest mom in the world!

Meet Mary

Mary Ottman is a Motivational Speaker, Leadership Success Coach & hilarious southern gal! With an MBA & a Masters in Leadership & Management combined with rising through the ranks of a male-dominated engineering organization, Mary has forged a 27+ year career transforming herself from electrical engineer to engineering executive. A true believer in living life to the fullest, Mary spent several years as a country singer/songwriter

 performing at famous venues like the Bluebird Cafe. She has hiked rocky trails in Africa and jumped off the top of a 108-story building! She is on a mission to empower women to become heart-centered leaders by being more confident, more visible, making more money and having way more fun along the way!

To learn more about how to Lead Your Life & Love the Journey, check out the latest at www.maryottman.com!

Chapter 3

Transforming Grief into Gratitude
How loss taught me to count my blessings

"Learning about the power of gratitude has changed my life. I fought it for a long time because I felt it was trite and insignificant, but when I found myself on my knees, gratitude lifted me out of my madness and taught me how to live a beautiful life despite the hardest of days." - Jennifer Sparks

My journey begins more than a decade ago. I was approaching the big 3-0 and was making promises to myself that by the time I actually turned thirty, I would have changed my life. You see, I was overweight, overwhelmed and overworked. I woke up each day praying to make it through the day so I could return to bed. Perhaps you have felt that way too?

I was married at the time and had two small children, working full-time as a teacher and working evenings on the business my spouse was trying to get off the ground. My marriage was flat lining and neither of us had the time or attention to address the relationship. Instead we drifted aimlessly towards nothing of importance. When we finally decided to go our own ways, I was terrified. I was now thirty-two. How would I support and care for these two small children and keep us all afloat? What would happen to us?

While I knew my future was uncertain, I also understood deep in my heart that staying where I was, doing what I was doing and living like I was living was not going to take me where I had once dreamed of going. I knew that despite my fears, I had to rediscover who I was and get back on track to living my one and only life. I think I finally understood that my happiness was my responsibility, but I had no idea what happiness meant to me anymore. Here I was with many of the things I had thought I always wanted, but I was miserable.

We divorced. I do not care what anyone says, divorce is a complicated, life-altering event. It involves letting go, forgiveness and grieving for the life you once had. But it can also teach you enormous lessons about yourself and your identity if you are open to evolving. I struggled for a long time. Life felt unfair. Happiness was elusive. I continued to drift, but I also had started to run.

I ran to escape dealing with emotions. I ran to punish myself. I ran to have time alone without the noise of small kids and my chaotic life. But as I ran, I also had sacred time to think about my life, which is a gift many of us deny ourselves. I began to pull myself together. I lost weight. I ate better. I was a better mom for my kids and a better teacher to my students. I was also learning about the simple things that brought me joy.

I used running as my "drug of choice" to help manage my stress and work through my thoughts and feelings. Eventually, I fell in love with all of it. I decided to explore triathlon and went on to complete two ironman triathlons. Life was great. I was fit. I was healthy and I was in love with my life. My children were doing well and life was beautiful.

Everything was as it should be. And then, life threw me a curve ball.

I walked into the living room and found my then 12-year-old daughter on the floor. Her arms were twisted into her chest, her eyes rolled back in her head, her breathing absent, and her face was dead body gray. In that moment, everything slowed and morphed into a time warp. I truly believed she was gone. I could hear myself screaming inside. Unbeknownst to us at the time, this scenario would play itself out many more times in the coming years.

As we would come to learn, my daughter had epilepsy. Her particular type of epilepsy often presents as puberty hits. And she was hit hard. This diagnosis changed her life, my life and left us struggling to make it through each day. She lost her independence. She lost hope for her future. She lost portions of memories and her desire to live life with reckless abandon. The side effects of the medications left her swinging from rage to complete sedation. She struggled with depression, anxiety and self-harm on top of the epilepsy, and precious teen years that should have been dedicated to her development were vaporized into a blur.

And I? I lost my little girl to all of the madness. Seizures. Memory loss. Mental illness. Rage. Fear. Medication side effects. It ate her whole.

I was her lifeline. Initially, I couldn't even leave her alone. If I left the room, the sound of a plate or remote hitting the floor left me wondering what I would find when I returned to her side. I found it difficult to work; my anxiety of finding her struggling for air left me paralyzed with fear that one day she would need me and I wouldn't be there.

We moved through the haze of days, stumbling like injured soldiers from the battlefield until one day we just couldn't anymore.

She had seized in the middle of the night and her bed alarm woke me. With a hit of adrenaline surging through my body, I tended to her and settled her back to sleep. I was already struggling with sleep deprivation from the weight of being her primary caregiver, and now I was unable to fall back to sleep. I sat with her, listening to her breathe. I drifted off to sleep...

Then she seized again. This time, the fatigue and stress twisted with my already frail emotions. I got her settled again and I slid down from the bed to the floor in tears, knowing that this disorder was going to pull us both into a vortex of despair unless something changed. I knew we couldn't keep doing what we were doing and expect to survive intact.

The following morning, I woke up feeling like I had not slept at all, but I possessed a clarity that had been elusive before. I understood at once that I needed to be responsible for what I could control. In this situation, that meant her medication compliance, doctor appointments, healthy meals, helping her with what she needed when she needed it, and my self-care. I knew I couldn't control her seizures, but I had some say in how we both showed up to fight this disorder. I knew we could control our reactions to what was happening, but we both had work to do.

I also learned how to ask for help. I had an awesome support system that wanted to help, but I didn't even know how they could help. After thinking about what I needed so I could show up more prepared to deal with my daughter's needs, I began asking for that. I had to get over the belief that if you asked for help you were weak. I was a single parent of two kids, working full-time, and I needed help. I had to become okay with that. When I did, it felt great!

The biggest lesson came to me when I found myself on my knees sobbing that morning. As I cried, I asked aloud, "What the hell am I supposed to do?" And the word came as a whisper, but I heard it.

'Gratitude.'

I didn't really know anything about the gratitude movement but recalled having heard Oprah talk about it years ago. I remember distinctively thinking that there was no way that gratitude could help someone who was truly suffering. I recall thinking the same thing again on this morning, except one thing had changed. I was out of options. I was desperate. I was willing to give it a try.

I began practicing gratitude in an almost superficial manner. I was grateful for the warm coffee in my hands, the sun on my face, and the days that were seizure free. But eventually, things shifted and the gratitude I felt became more profound. I began to dig deeper and as I did this, I began to wake each morning searching for the things I was grateful for. My focus on gratitude changed how I felt about everything.

24

I was no longer focused on medication, seizures, loss, rage and sorrow. I woke each day counting my blessings and I cultivated a response of gratitude to all of life's daily challenges. When my daughter seized, I was thankful it was a short one, or that she hadn't fallen and broken her teeth, or that she didn't require hospitalization. Because you see, I knew first-hand that things could have had a very different outcome. I knew first-hand she could aspirate and if we avoided that, I was grateful. I knew she could fall from stools, or smash her head on concrete when she dropped and if she hit the grass or seized in a soft bed, I felt we were lucky. Does this mean we didn't have bad days? No, this simply meant we were learning that a bad day didn't have to be a bad week or month. We began to find happiness in the moments between the chaos and we choose to focus on the beauty instead.

We are almost six years into this battle and my practice of gratitude has served us well. It has been my salvation. It has changed the way I look at the world and everything that happens *for* me. Gratitude seems small, but it is a powerful and mighty wellness tool. Gratitude has transformed my loss into something beautiful because it has given me the ability to finally see all the amazing things in my life that I had allowed grief to steal from me.

Rise Up Challenge

If you are finding yourself overwhelmed, particularly by something that you have no control over, consider how you can alter the way you react to events. Can you make a list of the things you CAN control and then focus on these things instead? This is a much more effective way to invest your daily energy. And please, remember that self-care tops that list!

Get over your beliefs that keep you from asking for help. Every successful person has someone in his or her corner. Coaches, spouses, siblings, mentors or a best friend can make all the difference in how you move through the day or week. No one really makes it through this life alone. Do not be afraid to ask for help, and do not associate asking for help with being weak or failing. When I started asking for help with what I needed, I was finally able to breathe again!

And finally, if you are drowning in despair and have no idea where to begin, start with gratitude. If you do not know what that means, I have written a book called *The Gratitude Transformation Journal* that outlines the impact that gratitude can have on your health and wellbeing. Start with that. Start small. Start with being okay with it feeling superficial and trite, because things will change if you stick with it. And when it does, you will understand the power of a gratitude transformation!

Meet Jennifer

Jennifer is the owner of SWIFTKICK Life, creator of the LIFEMAP™ Program and INSPIRE the FIRE Within Wellness Retreat. She is also the bestselling author of *WTF to OMG*, *Happy on Purpose*, *The Gratitude Transformation Journal* and host of the GET HAPPY NOW Podcast. She is a teacher, certified personal trainer, Ironman triathlete, single mother, and storyteller who is here to liberate the lost and the overwhelmed from the day-to-day

grind of mindless obligations so they can find their way back to happy!

She is a self-proclaimed personal development junkie who has changed her own life simply by changing her mind. Over 10 years ago, Jennifer experienced what she calls a "WTF Moment" and decided she was done with her current level of misery. She stopped blaming others for her situation and took full responsibility for creating change. She got seriously clear about what she wanted and began to use the power of focus, gratitude and curiosity to redefine her experiences.

Her mission in life is to help others understand that if they *step up and into* their lives they can move from WTF to OMG just as she did! You can find her online at www.swiftkicklife.com.

If you would like to download a PDF copy of *The Gratitude Transformation Journal*, go to http://tinyurl.com/gtjpdf and enter the code WOMENRISING to get the journal for free.

Chapter 4

Money Shame

How the stories you tell yourself can limit your abundance

"And it all starts with a trauma – it may be big or relatively small, but it's there, waiting for you to recognize it." - Michelle Cooper

All my life I've had a love/hate relationship with money. I love money and all that it provides, but at the same time it has given me incredible amounts of pain and anxiety. Somehow, it's the thing that I have focused my entire working life on. However, my knowledge and relationship with money changed drastically when I found myself leading a conference breakout session with the most heart centred, conscious entrepreneurs I have ever come to know.

I found myself in a circle with the five other entrepreneurs, where I was seen as the money expert. As we dove into this volatile topic, I realized there was something underlying each and every one of their money stories, their financial choices and their perceptions about money: a shame story. Shame that is attached to the money, shame that is tied to past mistakes which then led them to questions their judgment, their worth and the viability of what they were creating. For some, it led them to question if they were even actually meant to do the work that they knew in their heart and soul they were called to do.

As we dug into those stories, we uncovered the generational narratives they had carried forward and the limiting beliefs that had held them back. We started to heal the shame with forgiveness. I was able to give them permission to change their stories and their relationship with money so that they could move towards abundance. As this process went on, what became glaringly obvious to me was that my own story hadn't even been discovered. Even though I am amazing at working the numbers in business and I deal with money every day with my clients, I really had only scratched the surface towards working through my own money stories and limiting beliefs.

And then it happened, something that I never expected came flying out of left field; I was presented with an amazing opportunity to move my family to another country and experience adventure and a lifestyle that I had been working towards for a few years. However, this opportunity meant I would have to step up in a big way in my business and personal life. I was over the moon excited about this and jumped in feet first, but it meant that it was all going to be on me for a little while – the full financial responsibility for my family was mine for at least six or eight months. When the contracts arrived, I printed them out and was frozen with fear. Suddenly, I found myself so completely overwhelmed that I couldn't even pick up the pen.

What do you do when you are paralyzed? For me, I call in my circle. Over a few days, I worked through different aspects of the opportunity and came to understand very quickly that what was paralyzing me was my money shame story. Everything I had supported that group of entrepreneurs with was right there in front of me. I saw that even though yes, I had a really strong relationship with money, there were a lot of broken moments in my past and a lot of shame and stories that I was tying to my self-worth. Even though I feel I know money on such a powerful level, I had to go back and really uncover my own stories with it. That relationship starts with a trauma — it may be big or relatively small but it's there, waiting for you to recognize it.

For me, this trauma was the birth of my daughter, Holly. I had never imagined being a mom and certainly hadn't planned on it, so when it did happen I found myself completely out of my zone of genius. My go-to response was to convince my husband to stay at home with the baby while I re-entered the workplace — a mere eight weeks after giving birth. Now I think we can all agree that this is insane. Of course, I became ill with severe postpartum depression, putting my family's financial security in jeopardy. We recovered, but this was a narrative that I created in my life over and over again; I repeatedly put myself in this position and I recreated the trauma over and over.

What I can see so clearly now is that even though I work with money every day with my clients, and they are all experiencing expansion, if we don't get to the root of the shame that is affecting the majority of women in business they will never allow themselves to be successful nor can they create their legacy. Short-term gain is achievable by utilizing financial strategies in business, but long-term financial security will remain aloof until we go into the storm and get to the root cause of the shame.

Once we have discovered what that root cause may be, we need to forgive ourselves. The power of forgiveness is astonishing and it's something that I encourage you to practice continually. Whether it is a forgiveness meditation or the ho'oponopono – the Hawaiian forgiveness exercise – or something as simple as looking at yourself in a mirror and saying, "I forgive you," this is a key step. Complimenting this step is expressing and feeling gratitude. Gratitude is an essential component of forgiveness.

During this self-discovery process, several key lessons became the foundation on which I was able to move forward with my own abundance and expansion and support my clients' development as well.

Firstly, we interrupt the cycle with exploration – figuratively, we go into the eye of the storm so that we can avoid the paralyzing fear that comes from the destructive and limiting cycle we build into our lives around money. By discovering our root story – the generational and inherited money language along with our early experiences of money, we uncover the root shame story. This is the key breakthrough moment. We can use techniques like Emotional Freedom Technique, Reiki and conscious coaching to work our way through the trauma. Journaling this process is a key strategy to moving though it and beginning the healing process. For me, free writing was the most effective way to uncover the story and it came in layers – like an onion. Just when I thought I had gotten to the bottom of the story, there was another layer.

Secondly, we forgive ourselves for the past – our past mistakes, bad judgment, debt we built or maybe just stories we have carried forward unwittingly. By forgiving ourselves, we begin to release the shame. Forgiving ourselves is hard work, it can take a while and it is a journey. There is no quick fix but there are many approaches to forgiveness. It can be as easy as saying or writing "I forgive you". There are forgiveness meditations, exercises and rituals. I love writing a letter to myself and then burning it. That feels complete for me. Do what feels right for you but be prepared to spend some time in this phase - until you no longer feel triggered by the practice. Compliment every forgiveness exercise with an expression of gratitude. Incorporating gratitude into your day brings more abundance to your life and raises your vibration and energy. Forgiveness can feel draining, so complimenting it with gratitude completes it in a better mindset.

Thirdly, we rewire ourselves with a replacement story – what I call, our Wealth Universal Truth statement. When we uncover our current shame story, we identify what has been limiting us. We then replace that with how we want to feel about money, how we interact and how we handle money. By delving into our wealth core values, we discover what we are aligned with and how we want to show up in the money area of our life. Wealth core values are foundational beliefs about money that anchor our lives. My wealth core values are stability, joy and trust – these are the non-negotiable aspects of how I want to feel about money.

By creating our Wealth Universal Truth statement, which incorporates the statement of our wealth alignment (what core values you are in alignment with), we create and integrate a new emotion around money that fuels the life that we are striving for.

Another aspect of the replacement story is your abundance vision – what you see your life looking and feeling like when you are living your Wealth Universal Truth. Abundance visioning exercises are guided meditations where you are able to step into your vision of abundance. They are also journaling exercises, where you spend time writing about your wealthy future.

By incorporating abundance visioning exercises into our lives, we continually build our abundance muscles and move into our divine truth. Spending time envisioning what the future looks like when you are living in your Wealth Universal Truth is a key to manifesting it into your reality.

And finally, by creating awareness and accountability around our money, we show it the attention it deserves and we create the energy that attracts more into our lives. Having a weekly money date, where you check your bank account, your credit card balance, how much is owed to you and how much you owe others is a great tool of awareness. Setting your priorities each week around your money will move you in a forward momentum. Cleaning out your wallet creates a sacred space for you money. These tasks create clarity, awareness and accountability.

Looking back now, I can see that incorporating these four pillars into my life has allowed me to prosper. Using these practices supported me as I moved from shame to wholehearted living. If you are seeking more money in your life, I suggest you start by doing these four things:

1. Buy a journal and start free writing about your money feelings and the stories your family tells about money. Uncover the root shame story.

2. Forgive yourself for past money mistakes. Find one thing you're grateful for each day and three reasons why.

3. Create a sentence or two using words you feel aligned with to state how you want to feel about money. Spend some time envisioning your future self, one year from now. How does money show up in your vision?

4. Set a money date with yourself every week to review your bank accounts, numbers, credit cards, and business financials. As I confidently move into claiming my life in the new way it is rolling out, I realize that I am finally breaking a cycle and will thrive as the provider for my family. I challenge you to take on these four steps, live your full and wholehearted life and inspire others to do the same. Be intentional about money.

Meet Michelle

Pricing & Profit Coach, Business Alchemist, Speaker & Writer

Michelle Cooper is a powerhouse leader who inspires women to make more money and create change in their business. Michelle has worn many hats in her career, using her accounting designation to work around the world  in finance and business development from Citibank in London to Bali & Orient Adventures in Indonesia.

Adventure features highly in her life and business – this gal's a risk taker. As a writer, speaker, coach and entrepreneur, her goals are to motivate others to pursue their true passion, manifest their dreams and execute their vision in order to create the life they love living. Michelle loves travel and all the richness it brings to her life. Recently, she has been able to pack up her family and move to Mexico, all the while continuing to build her business and live a wholehearted life.

As a wife and mother, she understands the juggle that women in business do on a daily basis and believes that self care must be a priority (and can become your hidden super power in business!) By building a strong, supportive circle, women can rise up and take on the world!

Learn more about Michelle's adventures and how you can create a highly-profitable business that allows you the freedom to live life full out at www.michellebcooper.com.

Chapter 5

What We Can Learn From Pie Dough
A journey of self-discovery

*"Life is like making pie dough; it's messiest just
before it comes together." - Jo Ann Kobuke*

I love to bake, but pie dough has always been my nemesis. The flour flies all over, the butter doesn't yield to the pastry cutter or dutifully reshape itself into pea-size morsels. I'm always afraid I have the wrong amount of water. Just when I'm tempted to throw it all away and start again, I work the dough a little more and I'm rewarded for my faith and perseverance, because the magic happens. That messy mound of flour and butter becomes a disc of tender, flaky pie dough.

This past year I've realized life is a lot like pastry dough; it is messiest just before it comes together.

My motto used to be, "It's never too late". But as I approach my later years, I realize that's a bunch of BS. That's just what we tell ourselves so we feel better about the fact we're not doing what we really want with our life.

We tell ourselves there will be time later to visit Mom and Dad, take our children to the beach, create the business we've always wanted or take that vacation with our spouse. But what if we're wrong. What if there isn't any later?

The hard truth is that "later" can disappear in the blink of an eye. All it takes is a call from your doctor with your test results. Or that split second when you take your eyes off the road and the car ahead of you slams on its brakes. Or it could be a tragic decision made in the depths of despair and depression.

Why do we wait? Why do we bury our hopes and dreams deep inside? Why aren't we living the life we want?

It's because we're afraid of being hurt.

Most of us learn at an early age to avoid painful experiences at all costs. But when we duck and run for cover, we never learn the important lessons that pain can teach us. By refusing to risk painful encounters, we stunt our emotional growth and stop developing our strengths.

That's what happened to me.

Survival Mode

As a child, I was taught that you had to be strong. My parents were second-generation Japanese Americans. In their youth, they were forced from their homes, herded into racetrack stables reeking of manure and then imprisoned in the U.S. Internment Camps of World War II.

They learned that the world was a harsh place and in order to survive, they needed to be strong. They felt it was their duty to teach their children how to survive what the world would throw at us. They molded me to their value system, instilling loyalty, humility and the value of hard work, for which I am grateful, but it came at a high price. A price that I have been paying all my life.

There was no room in my parents' plan for a sensitive child who needed compassion and gentle nurturing rather than harsh admonitions. There was no room for a challenging daughter who talked back and expressed indignation over the unfairness she felt.

My parents couldn't handle who I was, so they tried to change me, and in doing so, they drove me into survival mode. At a young age, I learned to arm myself against the pain of being trampled on day after day. I created a safe, protective box that little by little became my prison. A place that kept me safe, but kept me from growing into the person I was meant to be.

It wasn't just my well-meaning, misguided parents that inflicted pain. There were tormented middle school years filled with the anguish of a gawky, nerdy, introverted wallflower with cat eye glasses that were definitely not cool back then.

There was the time I was walking home from school and the boy who had broken up with me the week before drove by. He stopped just ahead of me to pick up his new flame, lingering long enough that I had to walk past them, pretending not to care.

Oh, and there was the time I threw a party for my girlfriends and no one showed up but the girl from work who I had invited at the last minute. Talk about awkward and humiliating. The worst part was feeling like there was a big "L" stamped on my forehead every time I saw her at work.

And then there was the soul-shattering pain of a miscarriage and failed infertility treatments.

In time, my box alone wasn't enough to protect me from life's pain. I started adding layers of emotional padding in an attempt to insulate myself further. A layer to protect against the searing pain of rejection, and another when I was scalded by failure, and yet another when I was tortured by insecurity.

After a while the layers were piled on so deep I could no longer make out who I was. Over time, I became unrecognizable, a stranger to myself, and invisible to others. I was stuck as that frightened child desperately hoping to hide from the pain of life.

Birthday Candles

For my birthday this year, my daughter made my favorite chocolate cake. She put two candles on top, you know, the ones in the shape of numbers you put on children's cakes. The numbers were a 6 and a 4 . . . in that order.

She had been doing this for several years, but seeing those candles this year triggered something inside me. Next year I would be eligible for senior citizen discounts. Next year I could apply for Medicare. I was two years from being eligible for Social Security. AARP had been flooding my mailbox with offers to join. How the hell did this happen? I wasn't OLD!

My inner voice was shrieking. SORRY TO BREAK IT TO YOU HONEY, BUT YOU'RE GETTING OLD JUST LIKE EVERYONE ELSE. When are you going to get it? Those years are gone. You're not getting them back. There's no do over here!

Looking at those candles, I realized I had been cheating myself. I had spent those 64 years hiding behind a false front trying desperately to be "normal and nice". I had lived my life afraid of being seen, fearful of getting hurt, and petrified of being judged "not good enough". There were so many things I had held back from doing because I was afraid.

It was so tempting to stick my head back in the sand and ignore my thoughts. Why in the world would I want to shake things up and subject myself to the pain of self-discovery after hiding from it all these years?

Then I asked myself what would happen if I turned away? What if I continued living with the status quo? How would my life turn out?

Suddenly, in my mind's eye, I saw her, my 90-year-old self standing on my porch, ringing my doorbell. What had she come to tell me?

Would she reach up to hug me and thank me from the bottom of her heart for being brave enough to face my fears and overcome them? Would she tell me about her joyful years living a life of purpose, and how grateful she was that I had been willing to do the hard work that had freed her from regret and fear?

Or would she tearfully ask me why? Why had I let the years continue to slip past, leaving her to sit on the sidelines, watching the world pass her by? Why hadn't I acted when there was still time? Why had I doomed her to draw her last breath consumed by thoughts of the life she could have had?

What a wakeup call.

I had dreams of a life I wanted to live. I dreamed of creating a business helping other women avoid the traps that had derailed me for so long. I dreamed that I stopped caring so much what other people thought of me, and that I had the courage to take more risks and enjoy life more, but most of all I dreamed of a life without regrets. This was the life I wanted to give my 90-year-old self.

In order to do this, I knew I would have to peel off my layers of emotional protection. I would have to be seen if I wanted to create my business and that meant being vulnerable. I was terrified at the idea. But I was even more terrified of disappointing my 90-year-old self.

So I got to work.

I won't lie. It's been a messy and painful process peeling away layers and knocking down walls.

Sharing my struggles with you now, being in the messy middle, defies the conventional wisdom that says you should wait until you're through with your transformation to write about the lessons you've learned. But there are many valuable lessons to be had from right here in the messy middle.

I have to be honest. Change is every bit as scary as you think it is. There were times when I wanted to crawl into a hole and disappear. There were times I would just sit and cry. Sometimes I was so paralyzed with fear at the thought of taking the next step I would hide in my house for days, ignoring everything and everybody.

But that vision of my 90-year-old self kept me going. I knew that working through my fears was infinitely better than leaving this world with regret for a life not lived.

If you're reading this and you're not yet ready to make a change, that's ok. We each have our own journey, and we travel it at our own pace. You'll know when you're ready. Just keep listening to your inner voice.

But if you are ready for a change, if your inner voice is getting louder and louder, reminding you that time is slipping by, then I challenge you to think about your 90-year-old self. What life will you create for her? Will she thank you for your courage, for acting now while you still have time? Or will she shed tears over what could have been?

I hope you choose to act and to encourage you, I want to share some things I've learned from the messy middle.

Know that it's ok to focus on yourself. Give yourself permission to really live.

You have spent so much time being there for others. You've nurtured your family, your friends, and your job. But what about you? What have you done to nurture yourself?

Take time to reconnect with yourself. Who have you become? Do you like that person? If not, who do you want to be? What's stopping you from being that person?

Start day dreaming, in color. Think about the life you want. Create a vision board with images and phrases that bring your dreams to life. Put it somewhere where you can see it every day. Vow to take one step every day that will bring you closer to those dreams. Vision + Action = Success!

Support yourself with like-minded women who are working toward their dreams. Find your tribe.

Seek out like-minded women. It doesn't matter if their dreams are different from yours, what matters is they're willing to have dreams and to work toward accomplishing them. Their drive to achieve their dreams and to embrace the pain of growth will energize you to breakthrough what's holding you back. You need people who will have your back.

Reach out to women of all ages. Don't be afraid you're too old, be open to new ideas. Don't judge. It's that exchange of new ideas that will keep you energized and feeling young.

Stick with it! Your 90-year-old self is counting on you.

Make a pact with yourself to stick it out for a year.

Break the year into quarters. At the beginning of each quarter, write down where you are right then and where you want to be at the end of the quarter.

On a separate piece of paper, write down the steps that will get you there. Seal the first page in an envelope and put it aside. Tape the action steps to your mirror.

At the beginning of the next quarter, open the envelope and read what you wrote. How did you do? Look where you were three months ago. Where are you now? Celebrate your progress, no matter the distance.

Review what worked and what didn't. Use this information to make next quarter's goal. You'll be amazed at the progress you'll make, and how you'll change, but that will only happen if you keep going.

Don't fear the messy middle.

I'd like to say I've got it all figured out and now my life is tied up in a neat pink bow, but I can't. Not yet. The flour is still flying and my pie dough is still coming together. But I know I'm close.

There have been plenty of times when I've said to myself, "Who do you think you're kidding, you can't do this." Sometimes I would just sit in front of the television with a quart of my favorite ice cream and a big spoon, binge watching shows all day, too confused and depressed to even approach my computer. But after coming down from my sugar high, I would get back to work.

I have learned to be kind to myself when I stumble. I don't rake myself over the coals like I used to. I accept that it happened, I learn from it and move on.

I am determined to create a life my 90-year-old self will thank me for. When I hear that doorbell and see her standing there, she's going to wearing a great big grin on her face that will make the pain and struggle I'm going through now all worth it.

What about you? Who will you see ringing your doorbell?

Meet Jo Ann

Jo Ann Kobuke is a powerhouse speaker, thoughtful author and fearless leader for midlife women. She spent her professional career as a CPA. Fresh out of college, she chose the accounting world because that provided a safe and predictable career, but it was not a place her soul could flourish. Striving to fit into the mold of a good accountant, she tailored herself to the job but always felt like a square peg in a round hole.

It wasn't just in her professional life that she held back; she spent the majority of her personal life torn between her linear thinking  Type-A mind and her intuitive, truth sensing mind. She was afraid to show up as who she knew she was, an intuitive truth seeker, because she feared rejection and ridicule.

She knows what it's like to hide from view. She knows the feeling of constantly doubting yourself and questioning everything you do. But she also knows what it takes to shift your mindset and break through the limiting beliefs that imprison us.

She has learned that the story you tell yourself is the one that controls your life. She has chosen to rewrite her story to reflect who she is today, casting off what no longer serves her and stepping into her true gifts to create a vibrant, visible and joyful life.

Jo Ann is the founder of Midlife Rewritten and she has made it her mission to help midlife women rewrite their story, questioning old assumptions, crushing limiting beliefs and creating a life affirming new story that fits who they are today.

She uses her skills as an intuitive listener and truth diviner to help women recover from a lifetime of hurt and fear. She helps them peel back the layers that weigh them down, the ones that hide the beautiful soul within. She gently guides them through the chaos of change and stands with them as they transform into powerful, high vibration women who are determined to seize life and live it to the fullest. Women who will make their 90-year-old selves proud.

When she's not working, Jo Ann enjoys going to movies and plays with her two grown daughters, practicing yoga, and traveling. She's married to a fishing fanatic and finds herself constantly reminding him that while he's free to go with his fishing buddies whenever he wants, she will not be joining them because getting up at the crack of dawn to sit in a cold boat waiting for the fish to bite just isn't her cup of tea.

You can find her at www.MidlifeRewritten.com

Chapter 6

Find Your Magic

Awaken, reclaim and gather to heal the past and change the future

"Sisterhood is key to activating change; as we transform ourselves, we transform the world." – Flora Ware

Magic has always been a normal part of my life. I perceive magic as an energy and a way of looking at things, seeing things that aren't quite there — the in-between things.

As a young girl, I thought it was normal to hang out with faeries in the meadow down by the creek, and couldn't everybody see whispers of colour around other people?

Eventually, I learned this was not the case.

I delighted in being different though, so this was great news. It meant I had special powers. I intentionally honed those special powers when I was embraced into a friendly group of older women alongside my Mother. We met on the full moons and sat in circle together, singing and drumming, sharing stories and wisdom.

I was 15 and had my whole life ahead of me. I thought I had it all figured out. I respected the earth, lived attuned to her rhythms and if I followed my bliss it was supposed to all work out, right?

As a young woman on the cusp of adulthood, I felt that deep inside me, that I was destined for greatness. I sensed a calling from within saying I was meant to inspire people. I'd been on stage since I was six years old, and I knew I moved people with my performances. I therefore confused this deeper calling with what society refers to as fame. Unfortunately, I wasted the next 15 years pursuing an illusion of success.

At 19, I moved to the big city. I studied acting, but didn't finish the program. I then spent two years as a ski bum and backpacking around Central America trying to find my life's direction. Since I still felt my magic when I performed, I decided to go to Music College. Graduating with top marks, I re-entered the real world and struggled through my 20's like a good suffering artist: wanting recognition, waiting to be discovered and craving indication of success through fame.

On the outside, I was playing gigs, teaching chakra sound healing workshops, leading moon circles and performing in sacred theatre ceremonies at festivals. People perceived me as spiritual and grounded, yet I was frustrated with my life and felt like a fraud. I had my fair share of dark years with co-dependent relationships and chasing "enlightenment" through parties and drugs.

By my mid-30's, I'd spent tens of thousands of dollars on self-funded CD production costs and college tuitions, and logged countless miles on tours. I remember arriving home after a weekend of gigs on the road, exhausted. I had barely made a profit after paying my musicians and all the tour costs, which I knew by indie music standards meant I'd just had a successful tour.

I didn't feel anywhere close to successful.

Dropping my keyboard against the wall, it stayed there in its bag for two weeks before I set it up again to play. I was depleted and uninspired.

I knew I was talented. I knew people loved hearing me sing and were moved by my performances on stage. I also knew I hated having to pass the beer pitcher around to collect my own tips. I quit my dream.

I got a job in administration; securing a stable paycheck, a clean office environment and enjoying extended medical benefits. I stopped gigging. I even stopped playing and singing at home.

There is nothing more agonizing to an artist than feeling the pain of unfulfilled creative expression.

Morose and grieving, I drifted for a while, numbed from the hamster wheel of routine. Then one day, some old friends invited me to an outdoor dance gathering to celebrate the autumn equinox.

My heart lightened as we arrived and I was giddy to dance and play outside, playing with my inner child. As if no time had passed, I could see and feel my magic again. My steps were lighter, my heart felt expansive and I reconnected with my joy and my true self. I realized how disconnected I'd become.

During a medicine drumming session, I went into a deep trance. Guided, I asked my higher self, "What is holding me back?"

In my mind's eye, flames suddenly encircled me. I felt them licking my ankles, and then start to move up my calves. At first, I wasn't sure what I was 'seeing' and 'feeling' or what was going on. The flames continued to rise and the sensations intensified.

As I was consumed by fire, panic and fear overcame me unlike anything I'd ever known in this life. Images flashed by quickly; being aggressively pulled around, a crowd of people watching, looking down at mud. I could almost hear men's voices shouting and the echoes of dying screams while the flames engulfed me. I was filled with rage at the injustice of my murder.

Breathing deeply, I stayed present with the information I had just received so viscerally and painfully. This was the second time I'd experienced this memory, but over the years I'd dismissed it, doubting its validity.

"It really happened," I whispered, confirming it for myself. Tears began to flow and I shook with sobs, accepting and releasing the pain I felt.

This powerful moment reminded me that in the past, those who were considered to have magical knowledge were punished by death and silenced. Even though people are no longer burned at the stake, there are other ways that others try to silence our magic and stifle our truth.

You may not have the same kind of gifts that I have; we are all beautifully different, but you do have magic within you. You may be able to know what your spouse is feeling and the exact thing they need; you may be able to paint in a way that opens people's understanding of themselves; you may be able to guide someone out of darkness through your powerful listening skills; or you may be able to change a scraped knee into a mark of bravery with a simple kiss.

In that moment, I finally understood why I had been holding back all my life, expanding, then shrinking. I had been afraid to speak out, to fully shine, to embrace my true self and share my gifts — because the fear of persecution still lived in me.

I knew I had been carrying the fear for long enough. I chose to liberate myself from its grip once and for all.

Awaken

Since you are reading this book, I am sure you've been feeling the huge wave of energy as literally millions and millions of women are rising up at this time. We are remembering who we are, the ancient medicine ways and our women's wisdom.

This is an incredible, beautiful uprising. It is happening because the divine feminine is coming back into our remembrance, coming back into balance with the divine masculine. It is profound because as we connect into our true essence of who we are as humans, we are activating a collective remembrance of the true nature of life. When you awaken the Goddess within, you live with passion, power and purpose.

The good news is, we don't need to move away or become a nun or leave the people we love to walk a spiritual path and embody our divinity. We can wake up to our truth and our essence right now, and still live in the world. In fact, it's imperative for our future generations that we must.

I finally awoke to my truth in that moment dancing under the stars, and stopped trying to be somebody that I wasn't. Can you to remember who you were before society told you who you should be? Be still and listen deeply or access your essence and joy through dancing, drawing or journaling— whatever your heart is calling you to do so you can explore your soul. It doesn't matter how you do it, it just matters that you do it, and start to awaken again to who you truly are.

Reclaim

I considered myself a strong, independent woman. I thought I was smart and consciously awake. I would follow my true essence, at least for a while, and like all of us I would then get pulled in different directions and would make choices that led me away from my truth.

Yet, instead of taking responsibility for my choices I began to place blame: on my parents, my boyfriends, even my crooked teeth, and definitely on being Canadian as the reasons I wasn't successful and achieving my dreams. It was humbling for me to accept that I had been giving my power away, and realize that I was playing the victim.

Perhaps you have felt this too? Blaming someone or something as the reason we don't have what we want? When we place ourselves in the victim role, we are saying 'I have no control to change things'. I beg you to reconsider.

It wasn't until I accepted the fact that I alone was the author of my destiny, and stayed in that place of power, that my life completely transformed. Every day I must continue making the choice to be responsible for my circumstances, because every day I am presented with an opportunity to go back to blaming and feeling victimized.

To recognize how we put ourselves in this victim role we need to identify patterns of thought and behaviour. You should discover how this looks for yourself, because it shows up a bit differently for all of us. And don't judge yourself when you do discover it. Judgment doesn't empower us, and it keeps us disconnected from divine source. Simply acknowledge that you've been giving your power away and reclaim it, one day at a time.

It isn't necessary to analyze and figure out why, either, although you probably still will (I did). You may track its source to an overbearing parent who didn't empower you to make your own decisions, or unconsciously absorbing the patriarchal mindset of society that a woman must defer her power, or chalk it up to your passive personality.

Regardless, most of us have just unconsciously internalized the beliefs that we are not in control and 'power' resides outside ourselves. Neither is true. Reclaim your power, speak your truth and throw away your victim story.

Here are three questions to ask yourself so you can begin recognizing a victim mindset.

1. Who or what are you blaming for what you think you lack?
2. Who do you need to forgive so you can let the past be in the past?
3. How can you take full responsibility for your life circumstances from this day forward?

As I look back on how I could fully step into who I am and awaken the goddess within, it came down to reclaiming my truth, no longer suppressing the magic of who I am, and accepting the choices I made in my life. Ultimately, however, I know that to fully step into who you are meant to be you need to gather with other powerful women who are reflecting your highest potential back to you.

Gather

To accomplish anything, we need to come together. Biologically, women have an advantage to this, because we are innately collaborators. We lean on each other for support, sharing skill sets and working together to lighten everyone's daily burden.

Sadly, however, there can be a lot of mistrust between women.

This mistrust can come from many sources, for me it comes from my memory of a time when it was not safe for woman to gather. If you find this to be an issue for yourself, can you identify the source of your own mistrust?

Perhaps you saw your mother struggle with jealousy and compete against other women. Maybe you experienced your own envy and comparison that slowly poisoned friendships?

Sisterhood is key to activating change; as we transform ourselves, we transform the world.

Seeing your highest potential reflected back at you by other women who are learning, living and loving to their fullest is powerfully motivating and wildly inspiring. We simply must heal the sister-wound.

To do this, rekindle your old friendships that may have become distant. Refresh your connection with authentic, soulful conversation, or cultivate new friendships where you can be seen for who you are today, not the you from the past. Either way, create more opportunities for sisterhood in your life, and enjoy the healing and empowerment that it brings.

I envision our Granddaughters and Great-Granddaughters growing up in a world where pay equity is old news and government legislatures are gender balanced. I picture a future where girls grow up attending women's circles as a normal part of life. A future where we have healed the illusion of separateness and the need to compete, and a sense of sacredness for all life has returned.

This awakening, this uprising, can have a ripple effect that impacts families, communities and federal policies. We can no longer afford to be apathetic and lazy. The 'someone else will fix it' mentality must go. As the Hopi prophecy states, "We are the ones we've been waiting for."

Imagine the possibilities of our future if we all lived in alignment with our truth and power. Think of the magic that will be created as a result of each of us fulfilling our authentic calling that will feed our souls and change the world.

Rise Up Challenge

- Awaken the Goddess within you through journaling, dancing, art, or meditation so you can connect to the essence of your true self.
- Be vigilant in watching out for the ways you are unconsciously giving away your power, and then reclaim it.
- Join a women's circle or start a women's circle, and honour your friendships for the wonderful value they bring to your life.

Meet Flora

Flora Ware is a conscious dreamer, soul friend, Priestess and creatrix of Goddess Dreamschool. As an Empowerment Coach and Goddess Guide, Flora helps women hear their soul's voice, awaken the goddess within, and align their work, life and love with their unique feminine power.

Flora has been participating in and leading women's circles since 1993, and facilitating workshops since 2002. She brings her 20+ years of experience to guide women to create a life of magic and meaning and a successful business that is a true extension of who they really are. It is her mission to assist in the global remembrance of the divine feminine, as we heal patriarchy from the inside out.

In addition to moon rituals and deep conversations with her soul sisters, Flora loves hiking, swimming, dancing, singing and eating anything covered in pesto! She lives in Vancouver, B.C. with her wife and son.

You can find her online at: http://strengthandsoulwellness.com

Chapter 7

Happily Ever After
How it begins from within

"You are worthy, simply because you exist." - Sarah Madras

It was just another typical scorching hot summer in Florida. I was volunteering as a camp counselor at a local sleep-away camp. It was a weeklong adventure filled with canoeing, horseback riding and daily swimming fests during the day with the campers and marathon card games, pranks and Mayberry mischief at night with the fellow counselors. The camp experience became one of my favorite summer traditions over three years time. This summer, however, ended differently than all the rest; the end of this summer camp was the beginning of the next five years of my life.

On our last night of camp, the counselors stayed up all night sharing stories, laughing uncontrollably, and watching the sunrise.

As the sun began to creep up over the trees and cast its rays across the lake, the shy and soft-spoken boy next to me reached for my hand and asked me for my phone number. The moment was as innocent and sweet as young love from a 1950's movie. We began dating and quickly created our love story. We became each other's best friend and safety net as we navigated the transition of leaving our hometown and attending college. It was a relationship born from young love and led to life-altering lessons. The kind of young love where it feels so intense that you begin to believe you need each other to survive, as it is the two of you united against the world.

From the start of our relationship, there were roadblocks. He was younger than I. We went to different schools. I was his first girlfriend, an unexpected addition to his family on his last year before leaving for college. While creating a love with my boyfriend, I also tried to create a connection with his family. I tied myself into knots trying to earn their approval and get them to accept our relationship. I made it a point to make his younger sister feel included by inviting her to events we were attending. All the while, I was wishing and hoping that she would see me as the cool older sister-type, but instead she saw me as the evil wicked witch who was stealing her brother away from her. The fairytale, happily-ever-after relationship I had daydreamed about in my head began to tear and fade away.

I spent five pivotal years of my life trying to hold on to that fairy tale by being the person I thought they wanted me to be. We say yes to things just to get others to like us and end up losing ourselves in the end. I was no different, and kept thinking if I agree more and achieve more, then they will like me. If I am more thoughtful and giving, then they will love me. I constantly felt like

I wasn't enough. I felt alone, rejected and confused as to why they would not accept me no matter how hard I tried to please them. The deep sting of rejection became an unwanted companion.

When I attended family dinners, I was greeted by comments like, "Why did you have to come?" Or I wasn't referred to as a person at all and was met with questions such as, "What is she doing here?" My humanity as Sarah was being stripped away until I was "She." It was as if I was the adulterous other woman that broke up this family. I felt like I was walking around with the mark of "unwanted" branded on my chest. I felt tremendously hurt and betrayed by them, while still having so much love for my boyfriend. The conflict between love for him and rejection by them left me feeling confused and exposed. It felt like no matter what I did or who I was it simply wasn't enough. **That I was not enough.**

The Breakthrough

> *"Choose momentary discomfort over long term resentment."*
> - Brené Brown

In the quest to please them and gain their acceptance, I lost any resemblance of the confident, outspoken, independent person I once was and yearned to be again. I had shrunk into this small, quiet and weak version of myself dependent on their approval to feel loved. For years, I never even realized it was happening. We are so focused on wanting to make everything look perfect from the outside even when we are falling apart on the inside. I had become so skilled at making things look picture-perfect that I was able to fool my own family as well as myself to the pain and worthlessness I felt. It was like a slow death, one that was moving in such slow motion that no one knew it was happening, not even me. It felt as if a Dementor from the Harry Potter movies was consuming my soul, leaving my worth on life support. When, I looked at myself in the mirror I no longer recognized my own reflection. I had gained 40 lbs. from using food to feed my soul since I was so starved for love and acceptance. My reflection grew dull as my inner light dimmed. My voice became weak and non-existent from the fear of being misunderstood and feeling as if my voice was unimportant. I had given away my voice and unique gifts and conformed to this invisible person, because I thought maybe if I were invisible, then it would no longer make them angry that I was still around. I no longer felt safe to be me, because for the last several years, the messages I received was that who I am is not worthy of being seen.

I kept asking myself;

"How did I get here?"

"How did I allow this to happen?"

I wanted to feel happy and accepted. I wanted to laugh, play and enjoy life again.

But instead, I felt numb and the numbness was suffocating. I wanted to breathe again.

Breathe in joy. Breathe in love. Breathe in confidence.

I couldn't take the rejection anymore!

So I took a deep gasp for air and I finally asked his sister, "Why don't you like me? Why do you hate me so much?"

She told me she loved me as Sarah, but hated me as her brother's girlfriend and always would.

Her answer was the defibrillator that shocked my heart back to life, that cast the Patronus Charm to save my soul, and sparked the resurrection of my inner flame.

In this breakthrough moment, I realized their rejection of me had nothing to do with who I was as a person or anything I had done over the years. In that moment, I felt the sweet relief of exhaling. Her words granted me release from the prison of self-doubt I had locked myself in. **I WAS FINALLY FREE.**

Free from self-doubt.

Free from people pleasing.

Free from rejection.

I WAS FREE!

This freedom ignited my courage to let go of the relationship with the shy, soft-spoken boy from camp. That summer, I began a new love story. A story of self-love began by rebuilding me and creating my Happily Ever After From Within, because we all want to know we are worthy even when others reject us. The rebuilding is often the scariest part, as the pain we know can trick us into being more comfortable then the fear of the unknown future.

The Journey of Rebuilding

"There is a divine spark inside me. I am worthy of the space that I occupy on this earth. No one deserves more respect, joy, or peace than I. I have the right to speak, to feel, to think, and to believe what I believe. Those dreams in my heart, those ideas in my head, they are real and they have a divine origin, and so they are worth exploring. I am confident NOT because I am pretty or smart or

talented or kind. Those things change and can be given and taken." - Glennon Doyle Melton

Each day, I leaned into the discomfort of the unknown and summoned the courage to take small actions towards rebuilding Who I AM. I started taking my power back by speaking my truth kindly instead of being silenced. If I had a feeling, thought, or idea I spoke it aloud instead of hiding it inside. I learned what my boundaries were and practiced standing up for my beliefs and myself. If someone did something that was not okay with me, I would let them know that was not okay. I practiced the art of self-care by learning what brings me joy and re-fuels my soul, and I did those things. I learned to meet my own needs instead of being dependent on others to fulfill my needs. I was able to tame my inner mean girl so that I could accept and love myself regardless of my messy imperfections. I learned to trust my intuition and myself. I reconnected with my body through movement and mindfulness. Through my journey to resilient self-love, I uncovered my core belief that we are worthy, simply because we exist.

No one is more or less important than another. We are all equally valuable. We are all enough.

As newborn babies, we are born with the exact same pure, brilliant and untarnished worth, which means we are born equally worthy of joy, respect, happiness, love, inner peace and fulfillment. Our worth is not dependent on the approval of others, financial status, looks, accolades or anything else outside of us. No one can take away our worth without our permission. I had allowed my boyfriend's family to take away my worth and confidence. I gave them my permission by not stopping it. Knowing this, I owned my responsibility for allowing their words and actions to break me. Then I granted myself forgiveness, and forgave them. We get to choose if we allow people, circumstances and life experiences to make us question who we are and our value. I no longer looked outside of myself for approval. All the tools we need are inside of us. We just needed to learn how to access and strengthen them.

Knowing this truth felt empowering and unstoppable. I was able to let go of people-pleasing and fear of rejection so that I could fully embrace who I am, unapologetically. I learned that my worth is a birthright and that if we are all worthy then there is no special gift or secret sauce that I was missing. I learned that it is safe for me to be seen, heard and valued. That I can have loving and fulfilling relationships----and these relationships started with the relationship I have with myself. How can I teach others how to love me if I do not know how to love myself? I learned to love myself, and small step after small step I continued to build my self-esteem. I strengthened my worth to be so resilient that no matter the unpredictable challenges, pain, or struggles life may throw at me; it will not drag me down. The hurricanes of life can be swirling around me and it will not break me, because my roots of self-love run so deep and strong that I cannot be uprooted again. I can say this with such certainty and conviction because I know the truth of who I am and that we are equally worthy, simply because we exist. This core truth grants me the greatest inner peace, freedom, joy, contentment, and safety I have ever known.

Rise Up Challenge

Now it is your turn. I invite you to build your Happily Ever After From Within by knowing yourself and reclaiming your innate worth as the birthright that it is.

1. What are your core values?
2. What are your boundaries? What is okay and not okay with you?
3. How do you take care of yourself? What actions (small and big) bring you joy and refuel your soul? Then do those things!
4. What is your inner mean girl telling you? What empowering truths can you tell yourself to silence the mean girl lies?
5. What small step can you take to build trust within yourself and towards others?
6. What are you grateful for about your body and how does it serve you well?
7. Are you willing to believe the truth that you are worthy, simply because you exist?

Meet Sarah

Sarah Madras is a Relationship and Self Love Maven, Speaker, Author and Worthiness Warrior. Founder of Esteem Builders Coaching, she is known for her fiery passion that empowers people to embrace their innate worth and live their best life. She has a talent for thoughtful truth telling and authentic personal vulnerability.

Her transparency about her own relationship breakdowns and breakthroughs provides a blueprint for others to reconnect to their personal power, speak their truth, tame their inner critic, reclaim their worth and cultivate fulfilling relationships.

She combines over a decade of experience as a licensed mental health therapist with her coaching superpowers to help you feel seen, heard, known and VALUED in your relationships. She has seen professionally and personally how not loving yourself is the ROOT of all of life's challenges such as anxiety, depression, addiction, infidelity, divorce and low work productivity. The symptoms are endless--the root cause is the same. The solution is building a foundation of resilient self-love.

She is the boundary setting boss lady, call you on your bullshit, cheerleader in your corner girlfriend that we all want to have drinks with. She is an enthusiast of SoulSync moments and her core value of connection radiates to you. Her action-taker style of her signature programs Stonehenge of Self Esteem and Happily Ever After Formula gives you the essential ingredients for building resilient self-love paired with step-by-step activities for immediate implementation.

It is from her own self love journey that she has been able to cultivate soulful relationships with herself, her husband of eight years, their two young boys and extended family and friends. It isn't always easy. It is never perfect. It is always worth it.

Access your Happily Ever After at:

http://myesteemteam.com/coaching/

Chapter 8

The Labour of Your Second Birth
Reclaiming the story of your life – past, present and future

"Our second birth takes place when we let go of the narratives we were conditioned to believe, allow the old way of life and living to die, and step into a new life, one that is based on inner knowing."
-Katya Sivak

Imagine you had the possibility of two births of yourself in your lifetime? The first birth is the physical emergence from your mother's womb. During this time, we enter into a pre-existing family system and are dependent upon our caregivers for survival. Our beliefs and stories about ourselves, others and the world around us are shaped by our interactions with our caregivers, our communities and the society we live in.

My first birth and upbringing were ordinary. I was born and raised in a country where people have big hearts, but it is a country that, in my eyes, did not care much for its citizens. My mother, a brilliant woman, was a civil engineer and my father, an honest and hardworking man, was a teacher. They both worked hard in their respective fields, but they were not always paid for their labour or time. Money was often held back. It did not seem fair to me, yet I saw them staying silent despite this injustice and mistreatment.

They never said that times were tough, but some evenings I felt the desperation and hopelessness. There was this feeling in the air that there was nothing they could do but give in to the circumstances and other's demands. When I was thirteen and we were immigrating to Canada, my dad was told that if he could afford to move abroad, he didn't need his last six months salary. There was a part of me that was angry when things like this happened. That part of me wanted to speak up against the injustices I observed in my life.

However, because I did not witness my parents speaking up or fighting something that, to me, was so clearly unjust, I learned to stay silent. The part of me that was angry felt shame, too, because my desire to show anger was clearly not desired by others. Instead, I retreated somewhere deep and dark and wrestled with my emotions alone.

I was raised in a culture that insisted that a woman's one life goal should be to get married and have children. This was confusing to me because I saw that my country's legal system placed little value on protecting its women and children. While I witnessed signs of domestic abuse on the bodies of my peers and classmates, I knew it was best if I did not stir things up by speaking about what I saw.

I was raised in a culture that expected me to respect my elders, yet the government of my country held back their pension, ultimately forcing World War II veterans to beg for money and food on the street. This broke my heart and yet, when I spoke to my teacher about this, I was told I was "overly sensitive." I quickly learned that being sensitive was not a desirable personality trait and knew showing this side of me would result in shame and rejection. I hid and rejected my sensitivities.

As an observant and sensitive witness to these situations, I was unaware of the impact that these experiences would have on me as I grew older. As time moved on, these experiences and stories began to shape who I was becoming as a young adult. They began to form the tapestry of my own personal story and belief system. Speaking up was not ok. Staying quiet was good. There was no room for sensitivity, regardless of the trauma or injustice. I found myself caged in a deep darkness surrounded by voices of the government, my caregivers and my teachers, saturated in social conditioning about what was right and what was wrong. These same characters and voices dominated my being.

One day, years later, I sat on a park bench in Canada. I held my new baby in my arms, caring for him, loving him and nurturing him as he breastfed. A complete stranger walked by and stared at us. In disgust, he started to ridicule me, saying awful things about me as a wife, a mother and a woman. What he saw was me exposing myself in public, when what I was nurturing life, doing something completely natural and hurting no one.

I was offered this opportunity to speak up and instead I froze. I remained silent and the characters in my head began to speak up telling me that I was too sensitive, that I am not able to speak up for myself, that I should remain quiet.

At the same time, I also felt a quickening. My body shook and something inside me woke up. Although this moment might seem very insignificant to the outside world, I believe this was a moment that marked my second birth. My second birth came as a result of me listening to the story of my body, re-examining and reflecting upon what I had learned, how I had behaved, what beliefs, values, feelings, patterns and life scripts I had assimilated to, unknowingly.

The second birth is the moment we listen to the narrative of our body, re-evaluate the stories in our minds and become our own decision makers. Something magical happens when we begin to pay attention to our body's narrative and let go of the cognitive stories we were conditioned to believe. This magic is evident when we witness that patterns of behavior transform into patterns of choice. Our second birth takes place when we let go of the narratives we were conditioned to believe, allow the old way of life and living to die, and step into a new life, one that is based on inner knowing. When the second birth happens, our world gets turned upside-down as we take a look at different parts of ourselves and change our relationship with these parts. As a result, we change the story of our life: past, present and future.

For me, the second birth came when a new internal character emerged. I heard a voice that roared with rage. It said, "Stand up for yourself." The voice didn't urge me to just stand up to the man in the park. It called on me to stand up to other voices in my mind, the voices that were dictating how I should show up in this world and who shamed me for who I truly was. I called her Mama Bear and I wanted to learn about her and from her. As I began becoming more acquainted with her, I learned more about myself. I gave her space to be and learned to embrace her as she calmed down and started serving as a platform, from which I began to rewrite my story about who I am. I went from being a little obedient girl, a silent victim, to a woman who shows up in the world as herself, embracing parts of herself that others do not like or can not handle, and who unapologetically stands up for what she believes is right.

In the process of my second birth, I learned that I inherited my previous way of being in the world from my caregivers who taught me their own way of interacting with the world and reflected back to me their own perception of me. Their own way of being in the world was based on their past experiences, values, attitudes and beliefs. We can't blame them for that. As adults, however, we also have a choice to accept the gifts our caregivers offer and reject the pain. Of course as children, we do not have the capacity to sort this out and the lessons we are taught tend to stick with us. Often, we internalize the voices of our caregivers regardless of whether they are helpful or not. We nurture the parts of ourselves that our caregivers see acceptable, and we hide parts of ourselves that they deem undesirable.

When we are young, we comply with the desires and requirements of our families, culture and the world. As adults, if we do not make our own choices, we wander around our life lost. When we take a look at different parts of ourselves, we decide on what is good for us and what is not. With this new awareness we are reborn, and in the process of our birth, we rewrite the story of our life – past, present, and future.

How to reclaim the story of your life – past, present, future

Awareness offers opportunities for change; you can alter the parts of yourself and the story about your life anytime you want. In fact, we are able to be reborn many times in our life. My rebirth happened after the birth of my son. Some people find that they are reborn after a divorce, a tragedy, an encounter with death or a spiritual experience. Our rebirth begins with detaching from our old story. Then we get to know different characters, different voices that are characters of our story, parts of ourselves – the main parts, the quiet ones, the ones we consider positive and the parts we deem as negative. The final step is committing to the new story.

Detachment is important because it allows us to view our story objectively and helps gain fresh insights.

Embracing all of the parts of ourselves allows us to become more whole. It is easy to accept parts of us that are courageous, loving, empathetic and kind. It is much more difficult to accept parts that are anxious, angry, tempted or ignorant. We all have parts of ourselves that are confused, traumatized or lost. These parts must not be neglected or avoided; instead they can be addressed with kind heart and compassion. We often fight these parts of ourselves. When we fight them or attempt to banish them, they become our inner enemies that undermine our good intentions.

Finally, envisioning a new way of being and a new relationship with the different parts of ourselves, and committing to a new story, allows us to free ourselves from our habitual thoughts, feelings and responses that do not serve us.

To claim your story as the storyteller of your life, it is helpful to observe that there are different characters in your story. To identify these characters, begin exploring the story of your life from an emotional standpoint. What are some emotional highs and lows that stand out in your life? Ask yourself, "What are the parts of myself that I do not like or I am ashamed of?" These parts often show up as bullies in our heart. Anxiety, depression, self - doubt and trauma are voices that can bully & hurt us. For me, it was being sensitive. Is there a bully in your life that lives in your head and says many mean things to you? Identify and name it. What kind of things does it say to you?

The next step is to identify where this part of yourself lives in your body. Our inner bullies often show up in our head, but they can also occupy space in our bodies. Where does this bully live in your body? How do you feel its presence? How do you know it shows up? When I am being sensitive, I feel it in my throat. There is a lump in there that prevents me from speaking and it makes it difficult to breathe.

Once we know where it lives in our body, we need to spend some time with it, get to know it better. We can do this by becoming this part of ourselves, putting ourselves in its place and asking questions about how it feels, what does it believe about the world, ourselves, and other people, what it expects of ourselves, what does it want, what is it afraid of and what does it need?

Finally, we can consider how we want to change our relationship with this part of ourselves. Do we want to show it some tough love, banish it from ourselves, show it kindness or nurture it? When we change our relationship with these parts, we are able to change our story. For me, this meant a transformation from beating myself up for being sensitive to owning that sensitivity. I went from being ashamed of being sensitive to responding to statements like, "You are so sensitive!" with, "Yes, I am sensitive. Thank you very much for noticing!"

Today, being sensitive is the very essence of who I am. It is part of my intuition, my creativity, my passion and my ability to understand other people's pain and help them find their unique ways of healing. It allows me to rely on my inner sense instead of submitting to beliefs, expectations and ideas of others.

Rise Up

I call on you to pause for a moment and explore your current story and all the parts of yourself. Being aware of your current story and its characters will allow you to envision the new story you would like to write for yourself. Consider which story you are telling yourself about who you are, which characters play a part in your story and how you want to change the storyline. And then do it! Imagine you had the possibility of two births of yourself in your lifetime? Invite, welcome, celebrate your second birth and in the process rewrite the story of our life – past, present, and future.

Meet Katya

Katya's ancestors are from Siberia and Ukraine. They are farmers, artists, teachers and healers. She has always felt their endurance, creativity and wisdom within her. They are part of her story, and she is a part of theirs. It is her natural and deep calling to listen to peoples' stories. This led her to pursue a master's degree in Clinical Counselling and a career in psychotherapy.

Today, she helps people affected by trauma go back to the core of who they are beyond all thoughts and judgments to find their healer within, so that they can step out of the pain and into their power. She offers an opportunity for healing through body focused psychotherapy, neuroscience and intuitive presence.

She loves inspiring people through engaging presentations and brings a warm, genuine presence, soul and science to the stage. Katya connects deeply with her audience through the power of story and is able to guide them to their own truth so they leave inspired to listen to their inner wisdom and confidence needed to take the next steps.

When not connecting with people as a speaker or a therapist, she is out in nature - hiking barefoot, swimming in the ocean, foraging for wild herbs and taking her son, daughter and husband on many forest adventures. She loves mangoes, sunshine, essential oils and the sound of the rain. She practices heartfelt living, doesn't kill bugs and is a hungry reader. She is often daydreaming, cloud watching, star gazing and can be found talking to the trees.

You can learn more about her here: www.katyasivak.ca

Chapter 9

Don't Fit In – Stand Out!
Blast through the zone

"It's far less scary to shine your light than it is to blend into the background and fade." - Sarah Walton

'Comfort zone' – it's a funny phrase. It can be a contradiction. To be in a comfort zone suggests a happy place. For me, it conjures up a sense of feeling like you've come home, of being at peace, of a duvet wrapped delight of safety and predictability. Our comfort zone is really just that which we're used to experiencing on a consistent basis. If we're brought up in a family who encourages us not to show our feelings, stand out from the crowd or try new experiences, this pattern becomes our comfort zone. Here's the rub; we are all completely and wonderfully individual, with our unique experience of and interaction with the world. Those institutions and individuals who have attempted to encourage us to fit in and conform have not recognized that one size certainly doesn't fit all.

Not so long ago, I lived life well and truly locked in my own restrictive comfort zone. I held down a job whose politics I hated, but as a secondary school teacher, I knew it had a certain social cache, a respectability I was desperately holding onto, not knowing how to follow the entrepreneurial path of my dreams. Behind the scenes, however, there was an undercurrent of dissatisfaction that was developing into a tidal wave of uncertainty – where exactly was my life leading? It was this feeling that led me to taking a big, audacious step and to begin creating the life I desired. I was spurred into action by an idea I couldn't bear; what if I spent the rest of my life in the background, never achieving my potential? I shuddered at the thought. In following my dreams, I've learned that it's far less scary to shine your light than it is to blend into the background and fade.

To take you back, a defining moment for me occurred several years ago. My two children were still young, and I'd returned to teaching after spending some time off with them. I worked in a huge secondary school where I held a one-year contract. Working until 11 or beyond most nights, I was fitting in family life around my work. My husband had said, "Don't disturb Mum, she's working" so many times I'd lost count. There was a real disconnect between what I wanted to be as a mum and the life I was living.

On the day in question, it was lunch time. There was a knock at my classroom door. I was so desperate to have just 10 minutes to myself to eat my lunch (I love being surrounded by people and am not someone who wants to be on my own for long, but right here right now, I needed those 10 minutes). I sighed to myself. When in the last few years had I gone from feeling inspired and creative to overwhelmed and restricted?

I opened the door and there in front of me stood one of my pupils, shoulders slumped, head low. Here was a girl in a class who had been written off by others academically, yet was amazing. She had a hearing impairment that learning for her a challenge. Despite that, each lesson she would thrust up her hand to answer questions. She was hungry to learn, and wanted so much to help other pupils in her class.

To see her here, crumpled, her head sunk down occupying such a small space was a shock to me. She looked like a different child. She asked if she could tell me something but barely raised her head to look at me. So many scenarios ran through my mind and then, in a whisper, she admitted, "Miss, in this school I feel invisible." I felt as if I'd been punched. Here was a courageous girl who tried her best. She was polite and kind to others, but was admitting to me that she didn't feel seen or heard. She had been pigeonholed into a system where statistics that 'proved' how pupils were performing had become more important than educating the whole child and allowing creativity, imagination and self-esteem to flourish. She wasn't a grade-A pupil and so, by the criteria schools measure success, she wasn't even on the map. I thought of the banner plastered outside the building declaring that inspectors had found the school to be 'good with outstanding features,' nothing more than a sound bite for the local newspapers, and wondered when and why we had moved so far away from what really mattered. Here was a young girl losing herself trying to fit in, when instead she should have been standing out.

In that moment, I knew.

I wanted to tell my pupil that all her amazing gifts and qualities meant so much more than qualifications, that she also gave me clarity and awareness of my own position. The first life lesson this situation taught me was teaching wouldn't be my profession for life as I had once thought it would. I would no longer hold onto this job to present a picture of respectability to the outside world, but would show up authentically as myself and hold a space for others to do the same. This wonderful girl had her light dimmed by the very institution that should have encouraged her to shine. It was she and others like her who inspired the name of my own coaching practice – The Square Peg Coach. A beautiful painting and accompanying quotation by Erica Kathleen gave me the idea for that as a business name. It told of a woman who was tired of fitting into society's beige square holes and instead wanted to shine like the 'supernova' she was.

For the longest time, I'd been sending out mixed messages to the universe. I had been complaining about a profession which had come to rely on overbearing bureaucracy, yet I was still clinging on to it by my nails like a climber hanging on to a rock face.

In the end, the decision to quit was taken from me. I had been promised that my one year teaching role would continue. The hours of burning the midnight oil had all been worthwhile. They liked me – I thought. Maybe I could teach for one more year after all and I basked in the relative security of my continuing contract. That was, until the day a 20-something graduate was shown round our department. Her confidence surprised me; she had the air of someone who was looking where she would place her things. And then I saw a post on the school's website. The job I had thought was mine was being advertised.

I was sitting in the foyer of our school with several other

candidates all eager to show themselves at their best. I conversely felt flat, trodden on and misled. This was the last place I wanted to be. I felt like a fraud listening to the deputy head's PR talk, knowing the reality was so different. There were rumours circulating that the young graduate's dad knew our head – that made me feel worse. It was the end of the school year and all the best jobs had been snapped up. The interview date came to a close, and, no surprises, the self-assured graduate was awarded the position.

August came and went and for the first time in my life, I was left without a job. I wanted to feel the inevitable relief that would arise from stepping out from the façade of a respectable job. Instead, it was eclipsed by the fear which arose from wondering where my next paycheck would come from. I registered with an agency and was certain I'd receive a call, but, as I waved my husband off to work and returned from dropping my children off at school, I was left alone in the eerie silence of our house. I stood in the hall, unable to move. I had been used to a bell sounding every 40 minutes to signal a change of class, and like a Pavlovian dog, I had responded. Now, free to make time my master, I froze.

The second lesson was painful, but appropriate. I slumped down on the stairs, consumed by an uncharacteristic self-pity. I felt so overlooked and unvalued. Was this it? In my early 40's had my career been cut short? This was ironic, as I didn't even want the job, just to be the one who made that decision. What I was really wrestling with was the public perception of what I had done, the 'what will people think' syndrome. And then something happened: as I was sitting there, a sense of complete peace and light washed over me. I knew instinctively that everything was OK and understood what my next step in life would entail. I knew that I wanted to help other women acknowledge their strengths and abilities and live a successful life on their terms. No matter what their background, academic qualifications or experiences to date. I would show them that they had everything they needed to live a life they loved. In order to walk my talk, I would do all the things I longed to do, the things that made me really happy I would make a more prominent part of my life. I found a silversmith to train with. I signed up for a marathon and started running longer distances. I went on a personal quest to learn and grow. I wanted to push myself outside my comfort zone to experience more of life. I knew then I would work towards my dream of being a full time coach. I hadn't been in control of my teaching career, but I could certainly be in control of my happiness.

I soon realized that when we begin to declare our dreams, opportunities present themselves...but with them can also come challenges. One door may close before the next one opens. The path may take some twists and turns, but as long as you stay focused on the destination and don't waver, you'll get there. In the past, I held on to the safety net of my teaching job, and because of it I was staying stuck. The end of my job presented itself as a painful moment in my life, but I actually started to realize that what I had been given was a gift.

Finally, I learned the importance of honouring my own truth and following my dharma. Recently, this was shown to me while sitting with my Mum on the sofa. She has Parkinson's Disease which means that since her diagnosis, she stopped being able to climb the hills in her beloved Lake District. Cycling then became impossible when she could no longer turn her head, and subsequently fell off the bike. For her to make the journey around the corner to my house now, she had to be with someone else.

I was explaining to her that even though teaching should be an ideal career for a parent because of the school holidays, it actually encroached so much into family life in term time, spilling over so often into the evenings and weekends that I had come to resent it. In an attempt to highlight all the things I'd accomplished, she said, "At least you've travelled to Australia." I was stunned. The very thing she was celebrating with me in the present had been a bone of contention with her some twenty-odd years earlier. My parents thought that after studying for my degree, I should be settling down, getting a steady job and beginning my career. I realized now that this perception was borne of fear – a fear of what might happen to me in a country so far away, a fear that I wouldn't want to return home, a fear that if I didn't start earning and saving, I would never have the financial security they'd lacked growing up. You see, it was advice based on love, but advice that had been so wrong for me, all the same.

It is so important to recognize how we've showing up in this world. Are the decisions we make on a day-to-day basis based on fear, or love? Are we victims, or creators?

Bonnie Ware worked for eight years as a career for terminally ill patients. In her book *The 5 Regrets of the Dying*, she writes that one regret is wishing you had lived your life as you'd wanted. Not as your parents, teachers or spouse wanted, but YOU. Isn't it time to get crystal clear on exactly how you'd like your life to look? What makes you giddy with excitement? What experiences make you feel alive, rather than feel that you're sleepwalking through yet another day? There is a unique path for you. It's your calling. Can you hear its whisper in your ear? Whether you long to be a brain surgeon, a stand-up comic or to begin a dog walking business – it's OK. That is your thing and by doing it in only the way you can, you'll make the world a better place. If it doesn't satisfy your parents, partner or society in general, say, "Thank you" and do it anyway so when you're on your rocking chair in the latter stages of life, you can sit in the knowledge that you lived a truly lit up life and left a trail of light behind you for others to follow.

Rise Up

1) Think of a challenging situation you've experienced in your life. What happened? How did it make you feel? Now, with hindsight, what was the gift it presented you with? If your instinctive reaction is to say 'none' that's OK. After all, how can a traumatic experience be valuable? It may not be the event itself, but the way it allowed you to look at life. Did it make you live in the moment, appreciate those around you more or get rid of the things or people that no longer served you? There will be something, I promise. Now, when you train this muscle in everyday life and you look for the gift, the lesson in experiences that might at first seem hard will help you to align with those things which are really important to you. Make it a practice. Find the gift in the experience.

2) Make sure your intentions are clear. What exactly do you want? Focus on those things. Think about the language you're using. Are you talking about the things you don't want rather than the things you do? Create a vision board so that the things you really desire are in front of you every day. There are lots of great videos on the internet to guide you through this. I have a free video on my website, thesquarepegcoach.com.

I'd love to present you with an acronym I've developed to help me. I imagine a golden CASKET.

C – Create your ideal life. Really go into detail. What would an ideal day look like?

A – Ask for help. There are people who will have travelled a similar path before. The fastest way to get to where you want is to model their process.

S – Step up and take action. It can be all too easy to think about your ideal life and do nothing practical to get there. Small, consistent action every day is the way forward.

K – Know that you can achieve it. If you get the wobbles, the negative chatter, turn it around. Create affirmations that help you sustain your beliefs.

E – End- even when things get hard, and at some point they probably will, keep the end in mind and carry on.

T – Trust in the process, in the fact that you are supported and there are others willing you on to achieve.

3) OK. This may sound harsh, but as adults, our life is our business. We can't blame others for our current situation. I can say this as it has described me for so long – if you're a people pleaser, you'll be pushed and pulled around by others' expectations. Once you start filling yourself up first (which for so long, I felt was selfish), you'll be happier, more fulfilled and respected by those around you. Once you take that control, it's empowering. Wherever you're at now, your life can look a whole lot different in a few months if you really want it to.

Taking the above actions has allowed me to move towards my ideal life. I am pursuing a new career and moving away from a twenty-year career not with regret, but with hope. I took back control and created a life that consists of more meaningful connection with the people I love, following my path as a coach, speaker and author. All of this meets my needs in such a magical way...and you can do the same too.

Meet Sarah

Sarah is a passionate change-maker who believes that connection, kindness and following your own unique path are the keys to

making our world a better place. She believes that society and the education system sometimes try to shape us into a round hole when she knows it isn't fitting in, but standing out that will make all the difference in your life.

At a primary school parents' evening, her Mum and Dad were informed that although academically things were fine, her response to humour was loud belly laughter. This was unlike other girls, who would snigger behind their hands. To this day, Sarah is an advocate for loud belly laughter.

Her biggest achievement is being a Mum to two amazing teenagers who teach her to see the world through their eyes, leading to uncovering daily life lessons.

She has co-authored a book called *Women Rising*, and a work of teenage fiction is in its final daft.

She has created 'Living Vision Board' workshops for women who want to maintain a high energy around their goals. Her favourite part is the last half hour where participants witness each others' amazing life visions.

Sarah loves to challenge herself and others to blast through their comfort zones and in doing so, gain a new perspective for their life. As part of this quest, she has run three marathons and has added a wing walk and swimming with sharks to the list of experiences she wants to create.

On stage, Sarah loves nothing more than to reconnect her audience with their purpose and give them permission to grasp it with both hands. It is time for us all to realize we are not meant to fit in, but rather we are meant to stand out. When we do this, we will live our life on our terms and be an example for others within our circle of influence.

You can find out more about Sarah's work by emailing her at sarah@thesquarepegcoach.com.

Chapter 10

Creating the Perfect Storm Within

How to use the elements of nature to heal and transform your life

"Energy is everything, and everything is Energy." - Cindy Starlight

I have always believed that I needed to work hard, be responsible and take charge of my life, or in some way I would be worth less. I lived with this belief every single day of my life. I don't recall making a conscious choice to live this way, yet I do remember many times feeling angry, sad and trapped by this belief. When I would recognize this conflict within myself, I would push it away and move on to what needed to be done.

I remember working hard from the time I was a young child. I landed my first job at 10 and was proud to be earning a paycheck when barely in my teens. I was doing my part to support my family and myself. Fresh out of college, I had an opportunity to show up and demonstrate my skillset and work ethic, which eventually helped me earn my way up to a top executive position in Finance in New York City. The issue was, working hard became my identity and I used it as a way to define myself because I had neglected everything else. Work had consumed my spirit and me.

Yes, there were nudges to change *things* along the way. I, however, ignored the light, airy breeze of the intuitive whispers until they grew stronger and pulled at me like currents under an ocean wave. Still, I was lost in the noise of hard work. I didn't stop and listen. Had I tuned *into* myself, I would have felt the fire stirring… but we all know that when we *don't* pay attention to the whispers, the correcting force gets stronger and louder until we have no choice but to pay attention. I *still* continued to ignore the nudges.

Then a correcting force made me pay attention. Call it fate, destiny or divine intervention; it changed the *trajectory* of my life.

In a situation I can't describe properly within this context, I found myself physically trapped under a solid mahogany table, pinned to the marble floor. I was unable to do anything but cry for help. In that moment, my world spun, my mind buzzed with disjointed thoughts and I heard myself saying, "I'm listening now!" I was tuning in. I was paying attention.

For the next two and a half years, I continued to suffer excruciating pain through my body. Doctor visit after doctor visit yielded a mixed bag of *diagnoses*. I had no answers, so I chose to surrender.

However, one doctor insisted that I see a top specialist to make sure nothing serious was missed. He was so adamant that I went to the appointment. As I sat in the little room post consult, I thought about the rest of my day, not expecting a diagnosis of any kind. When the doctor came back into the room, I was informed I had CRPS, a rare chronic pain disease.

Having been previously misdiagnosed with this condition, I was well aware of the living death sentence I was being given. The room spun as I heard him saying, "There is no cure, but we will do our best to make you comfortable."

Comfortable? Comfortable how? Comfortable as I slowly faded into a crippled, pain-filled body in a wheelchair, praying to die?

I returned home devastated by the news. By nightfall, I was crumpled on the floor in the fetal position, sobbing and begging for answers. "How could this happen to me?" "Why me?" As I sobbed and broke into a million pieces, I felt things shift and a new strength deep within me began to surge forth. I would not let this disease become my identity. I would champion for myself and I would choose light. I would not let the darkness overcome me, and I would move forward with hope. I would not let this disease *define me*.

In order to know light, you must have experience with darkness. To know freedom, you must understand struggle. To embrace *love*, you must have held fear. It is these elements that work together to create the perfect storm in our lives, that which allows us to embody significant power, yet be humble and gentle and choose light and not destruction.

If you find yourself lost and consumed by struggle I invite you to

RISE UP and embrace the change you need that can set you free.

Surrendering to Stop Sinking

Firstly, surrendering and letting go can feel scary, as you are venturing into unknown territory. For example, if you are in an unhealthy relationship, it becomes what you know and it is comfortable to you. There is a sense of certainty in the dysfunction and drama and you know how to operate in this environment. Whereas if you let go and move on and away from this dysfunction, you move quickly into foreign lands where you do not know the rules of the game- this feels uncomfortable to you. The bottom line is, change can both be scary and exciting.

Imagine being in the ocean; if you kick and flail your body around, you'll most likely sink. If you relax your body, though, and stretch out flat, facing upwards, you notice that you'll begin to float. The more you let go of the tension and surrender, the more you'll be able to float.

Now imagine doing the same for yourself. Relax your body, your mind and your emotions, and let go. Surrender. Surrender to what is, to what's going to be. Just breathe and surrender, let it all go. The more you can let go, the more room you have within you to allow something better to fill the space.

If you feel like you are starting to sink and are unable to relax enough to surrender to what's aligned to your inner heart, I want you to stop and breathe. Take three deep breaths, inhaling through your nose from deep within your stomach and exhaling through your mouth, and do so with sound. *Using sound* actually helps to get that energy moving, because that's what you want, to let go of any stuck energy that's keeping you from moving forward and keeping you from letting go. With each inhale, breathe in a powerful affirmation and with each exhale, release a potent surrendering of something that is keeping you from letting go. For example, you could say on the inhale, "I'm breathing in courage" and on the exhale "I'm releasing all fears".

Moving into the Eye of the Storm

Now that we have been able to let go of feelings and emotions that we have been holding onto for so long, and now that we have been able to surrender to whatever is happening, we can finally start to move through our pain, not against it.

After my wake up call, I went through my own cycle of different emotions, from being totally pissed off, to dealing with physical pain, *grieving the loss of my old identities*, to holding the sadness, to facing despair, and then back to hope again. We need to allow ourselves to feel, unapologetically and without explanation. I needed to learn how to feel in order to heal.

As I started to feel all my emotions, getting into the heart of them, I started to make better choices for myself. I needed to be able to use the passion of my emotions to fuel myself in a positive direction; a direction that supported me, rather than hindered my efforts.

I began to raise my vibrations, explore my intuition, connect with The Elements of Nature and learn to balance them & find my way into the Eye of the Storm. The *center* within the storm is like the *center* within us- this is where we connect with *a tremendous source of power*.

With this new awareness of how a connection and a relationship with The Elements of Nature could help me heal, I began to discern between how Earth, Fire, Water, and Wind could play a role in transforming my life. I began to lean on the Elements when I started to feel out of balance. I then drew a power from this knowledge to move into a new way of living.

Now equipped with this incredible wisdom, I began to deepen and refine my work with the Elements. I have discovered so many connections between Nature's Elements and life, and how we can use them to heal and move forward through exploration and utilization.

You can use Nature's main Elements of Earth, Water, Fire and Wind to help you move through trying times *and to enhance good times.* Below, I have outlined briefly how you can apply these building blocks of life, along with the gifts each offers you when you feel out of balance in life.

Nature's Element of Earth

Nature's Element of Earth is a stabilizing force and helps you to be more grounded and effective in your physical world. It's useful in the manifestation and process of bringing ideas into reality, especially where physical survival is needed, like clothes, food, security and all the means to maintain our physical form. The Earth Element is related to our Earth Star Charka and Root Chakra and our Physical Body including the bones, *muscles, and tissues* of our body.

If you are feeling ungrounded, go for a walk outside or just step on the ground barefooted. This activity will assist you in connecting more with the Earth Element and leave you feeling more stable during times of turmoil.

Nature's Element of Fire

Nature's Element of Fire assists you in aligning your actions and energy with anything you are choosing to create. Working with Fire fuels your life force, illuminating your creations and transformations. This Element allows us to radiate our brilliance, claim our personal power and let our light shine brightly. It allows us to embrace our passion for life fully. The Fire Element oversees the Sacral and Solar Plexus Chakras and the digestive, endocrine and meridian systems within our body.

If you are feeling like your energy or passion is depleted, Fire up your creativity! Color, draw or paint using vibrant colors on blank paper. Add objects like stones, flowers and anything that makes you feel joyful. Allow yourself the freedom to create. You could also watch a sunset and take in the brilliance of this essential element.

Nature's Element of Water

Nature's Element of Water helps distribute energy within the body and improve your self-esteem. It is critical to our vitality. It governs our emotions, intuitions and ability to communicate. The Water Element correlates our Heart and Throat Chakras, our Emotional Body and is related to the water and blood of the Human body.

If you feel as though you're not able to express your emotions and you're feeling suppressed, release them by dancing around to your favorite songs, enjoying a salt bath or writing down your feelings in a journal.

Nature's Element of Wind

Nature's Element of Wind increases your ability to think clearly, align your thoughts, mindset and your belief systems. The Wind Element is relevant to our Mental Body, connects guidance from the Spirit World, Higher Realms and our Dreams to our Conscious thoughts, Intuition and Prayers. The Wind Element is affiliated with the *Third Eye* and Crown Chakras along with the breath and the respiratory system within our Physical Body.

If you are feeling unsure of your vision coming into reality, then I want you to spend time imagining your desired outcome as if it has already come true. Close your eyes and see it already happening; feel yourself in that moment and hear the sounds around you. On a regular basis, think only thoughts of it already coming true. You could also keep a dream journal & write down all you can remember, even if it doesn't make sense. After, look up the meanings of the different items or symbols and see if anything resonates with you or look to see a pattern. Come back to your dream journal at a later date and see how your interpretations progressed.

Enter the Storm

Understand that your healing and transformation process will take place in the eye of the storm. Using the elements to help you stay balanced in that storm is essential, otherwise placing yourself in it can be a difficult experience.

However, there is also one other thing that cannot be ignored, and that is your choice to always choose light before the darkness chooses you. This is a conscious choice you make, thereby becoming your own advocate to deflect the labels and beliefs others may try to attach to you. Define and choose your own identity. Do not give that power away to anyone. Embrace it. *Accept and invoke* the light within.

Yes, there will be fears and darker times. Yes, there will be challenges and struggles and yes, there will be trials and tribulations. Always choose the way of the light. Choose the light within yourself and allow your inner spark to rise up, allow your light to illuminate your inner self to others and to the world. You must honor, cherish and appreciate what choosing light *grants* you.

If you feel yourself starting to slip into the darkness, I want you to repeat the words "I'm the Light." Do what you can to bring more light into your life, even if it is in small actions. Knowing that Dark (Fear) and Light (Love) can't be in the same vicinity; your role is to bring forth anything of a higher vibration and the Darkness/Fear will have no choice but to dissipate.

As I reflect on my own journey, I know that sometimes the most rewarding learning takes place in the darkest struggles. Failure to listen to your intuition and gentle whispers may put you on a more challenging path, but *for myself, it was* also one of greater exploration of my inner self and discovery of true Divine Path of Purpose.

My own journey has taught me what it means to be almighty powerful and helpless all at the same time. It has taught me to be conscious of my thoughts, actions, behaviors and patterns, as they are Energy in motion. I learned to listen to the nudges, to surrender and to create the perfect storm by *incorporating* the elemental energies around me. In doing so, I learned to harness their powers and my power within, enabling me to benefit from the *harmonious* combination of all Four of Nature's Elements at the height of their power, existing in the eye of the perfect storm.

It is your time, now, to move towards the eye of the storm to access your true potential and power. Embrace your Energy, have reverence and gratitude for your energy, for Energy is everything and everything is Energy.

Meet Cindy

Cindy Starlight is an Advanced Crystal Master and Certified Crystal Healer, Reiki Master and Certified Intuitive Strategist. She also has earned several other certifications in Energy Work, The Elements of Nature and The Plant and Animal Kingdoms.

Cindy also has a Bachelor of Science in Psychology. It was during her time as a student that she was first introduced to the concept of how vibrations and frequencies affect human behavior. This ignited a passion that catapulted her into a life dedicated to learning how different vibrations and frequencies affect human beings, and understanding the relationship between the human world and the energetic world.

Now, she incorporates Nature's Elements of Earth, Wind, Fire and Water into her work because she knows that each Element is a part of who we are, and there is great power in working through and in harmony with the Elements.

By combining several different modalities in her Spiritual Toolbox, she is able to facilitate healing each person as a whole body Being (physically, mentally, emotionally, spiritually.) Her often-sought out private sessions are heart-centered and vibrational, which leads her clients on a truly transformational healing journey where she is able to connect with her clients' higher self and energetic field. Using her unique skill set coupled with her extensive knowledge, she provides her clients with a specialized tailored healing experience.

Cindy also uses those skills to provide others with amazing meditations, products and courses that she teaches others how to utilize The Mineral Kingdom and The Elements for themselves.

Cindy's lifelong passion for crystals and metaphysics and her dedication for knowledge brought all her seemingly divergent interests into one path of healing.

Cindy can be found online at www.CindyStarlight.com.

Chapter 11

Redefine Normal

How a special needs child can teach you how to live life

"We didn't lower our expectations, we adjusted them. We made our expectations and decisions fit both the situation and our child." – Wendy Andersen

Normal: (1) the usual, average, or typical state or condition [n] (2) conforming to a standard; usual, typical, or expected [adj.]

We live in a world where everyone is trying hard to have the normal home, normal family and normal life. The world has created expectations of who we should be as parents, who our children should be as kids and has set standards so if we don't fit that mold, something is wrong.

For example, when I was pregnant with my first, people would ask me about my child and I would reply with the typical response,

"Boy or girl, as long as they are healthy." That didn't last too long, because it didn't feel right. We knew regardless that healthy or not, we would love our child to pieces.

A few months later, our son was born 15 days early. He came out yelling like the strong little man he has become. Everything was wonderful with our healthy little boy. Then about six months later, everything changed.

I received a phone call from my mother-in-law. It was a Friday, and I remember her saying, "I don't think something's right. Can you come home?" Slightly panicked, I rushed home, wondering what could be wrong. When I got there, he was just waking up from a nap. I couldn't see what she was talking about as she tried to explain it to me. It wasn't until a few hours later when I finally understood. Yes indeed, something wasn't right, so off we went to the pediatrician. She too saw what we had been seeing and said, "You have two choices, we can schedule him an appointment with a specialist in a month or so, or we can check you into the hospital right now." Hospital? Right now? It didn't seem like much of a decision to us. We were checked into the hospital within the hour.

I'll admit, there were tears on the way over. Like most first time parents, you never really know what is normal, but we knew that what we were seeing was not. There were a couple days of tests, blood draws, MRIs, EEGs and wires connected all over the place to our little boy. We would comfort him through his cries from being poked, prodded and the annoyance of having nurses and doctors non-stop with their hands on him. He was still happy, mind you, but these "episodes" as we would call them would come over him and he couldn't control his head dropping for minutes at a time

CHANTELLE ADAMS & OTHERS

(but really seemed like hours to us.) We would push the nurse's call button when they would start, only to feel like we were in some episode of Grey's Anatomy where all the interns come rushing into our room so they could see and experience what we now know were infantile spasms, a debilitating seizure in children.

My husband and I spent those nights in the hospital talking more than sleeping, thinking more than eating and pondering the events of the last 36 hours. You see, our seemingly-normal life was about to get redefined.

I remember the neurologist coming into our room after a couple long days of tests telling us that the good news was, they knew what was causing these infantile spasms. The bad news was, it was a condition known as Tuberous Sclerosis Complex (TSC). He advised us to go to a specific website to learn more about the condition, and not to Google it. He wanted us to get the best, most reliable information available.

At this point, we had many decisions to make. Yes, one of them meant that we eventually Googled tuberous sclerosis. The doctor told us not to, but really, how bad could it be? We saw the grim stories, and with them, we saw what life could potentially be like for our little boy. We saw the debilitating effects of infantile spasms. We found the stories he was trying to protect us from.

We looked feverishly for answers to all our questions only to learn there is still much unknown about the disorder. Finally, tired and exhausted, feeling a little helpless, we shut our computers down, turned off our phones and my husband and I held our little baby through another cluster of seizures. We thought all we could do is wait for a newly approved medicine to see if it worked.

We were overwhelmed. We hadn't really considered the implications of a life-long disorder. Something that couldn't be "cured". Something that was going to impact our son, his future and our lives every single day.

Shortly before being dismissed from the hospital, I remember looking at my husband and realizing I was a few steps behind in my processing of the last few days. I was so thankful for him allowing me to go through this at my speed and on my time (just as he has always done).

We had both realized, in our own time, that we got to choose how we handled this. That realization made all the difference.

We realized we could lie down and stay down because now we had a son with a very rare disorder, or we could rise up and love him like we always had. We could care for him and get him the best medicines, the best doctors, the best therapy and always be asking ourselves, "What's best for our son?" We had a choice, and at that moment, my husband and I made a choice to Redefine Normal and Live Life, loving our son just as we had always done!

We all have a choice

Our first and most valuable lesson was that we had a choice to do what was right for our family.

We didn't lower our expectations, we adjusted them. We made our expectations and decisions fit the situation and our child. We chose our expectations and didn't let other parents, physicians or experts (although we did consider their knowledge), in-laws or my own parents decide this for us.

We made conscious decisions about our family and our lives, and once we embraced this lesson, life got easier. Our decisions became less about what was expected and "normal" and more about what was right for us!

The same is true for you! Claim this power. You get to decide and make choices. You get to decide what works and what doesn't, and when to try something else.

You have the power to choose. To decide, and most importantly, discover what "normal" looks like in YOUR life for YOUR family.

We all have choices. They are OUR choices. It doesn't matter what anyone else thinks, suggests or recommends. We get to decide what's best for our lives and our children and in each situation. WE get to choose how to Redefine Normal.

Get comfortable with the uncomfortable

I was recently telling a friend about an experience when my son was really having a hard time at a mall. He was 5, and recently diagnosed with level one autism and there were sensory issues that we hadn't quite figured out. He was having what most people would call a massive fit, and in their eyes, "acting out". I knew he was on sensory overload from all the lights, sounds and stimulus. My friend said to me, "Weren't you worried about what everyone else in the mall was thinking?" The word NO automatically jumped out of my mouth.

We made a choice that day in the hospital that we would do what was best for our son. In the moment of his panic, his over-stimulation, I wasn't worried about what everyone else in the mall was thinking because it didn't matter. What was important to me was what his needs were and how I could help.

Within 5-10 minutes, what probably seemed like an eternity to other people, I had him up, settled down and on my back for a piggy back ride to go about our day just like we had before.

Was this situation uncomfortable? Yes, but in the uncomfortable moments, I chose to see a little boy who couldn't process the stimulation around him and a little boy who needed his Mommy. It didn't matter what anyone else thought, they don't know our situation and our story. They don't know what's normal (for us).

Being a team takes hard work, but you know when it's right

We do not have everything figured out nor do we have all the answers, but that day in the hospital we did decide one thing; my husband and I decided that we were going to be a team and work at this together.

It takes work and honestly, it's hard work! Occasionally, we are at different places than one another with a decision or thought process, but that's ok. We've embraced the fact that we process events at different rates and respect that eventually, we'll both have a decision. We work on understanding where we each are in the process and look to assist with fears, concerns, confusion and stumbling blocks.

We also work on building a medical & support team. We work with Doctors, Specialists, principles, teachers, paraprofessionals, and therapists. Having a strong team around to support and assist is integral to success. Others won't always get our situation or us because they aren't living it 24/7 and that's ok; they don't need to. What they do need to get is we're doing what is best for our child. We're not always on the same page, but we all have our son's best interest at heart.

We share our son's story with others so they understand where we've been and where we are going. We show them a picture of him on a ventilator after a massive febrile seizure so they know the fear we have gone through. Hearing the doctor shout, "Get the crash cart!" never leaves your mind, and when we drop our son off to school, that image sometimes comes back. Most people really have no idea what our life is like other than what they witness from afar, but having our team helping our son is what makes all the energy and effort worth it.

We've also chosen to love those around us. Friends and family see something on the internet and want to share it. It can be easy to get upset; how do they think they are helping? Instead, we see love. We see someone who genuinely wants to help, but doesn't know how. It's an act of love, and them trying to help in any way they can (even though they may not understand.)

This is also one of the biggest investments you could give your family; a loving partner and growing team who is ready to answer the call. When it's working well, the world is right and when the team needs to adjust, you adjust. It's about choices. We choose who is on our team, and when it's right, we all know it's right.

In closing, we live in a world where everyone is trying hard to live by the world's definition of normal; the set of expectations of who we should be as parents and as a family. I believe in a world where normal is relative to you and your situation. A world where each family knows their own kids. A world where parents think, "What's best for my child?" A family that is comfortable with the uncomfortable and builds a team around them to set sail for the most amazing journey in this life that they are choosing to live, love and embrace.

Remember, you have a choice. It's time to Redefine Normal and share what "normal" really is, because God doesn't give special needs kids or any kid to special parents. He give them to just the right people. Redefine YOUR Normal.

Now it's your turn to Redefine Normal

1. Is there one or more decisions in your life that you are allowing others or society's definition of normal to be made for you? Once you come up with this, consider how can you adjust to have things be in your family's best interest.

2. Think of an uncomfortable situation you have been in and give yourself three ideas of how to embrace the feeling of being uncomfortable so next time, you can feel more comfortable.

3. In what way can you strengthen the chemistry around your partner and/or team that you hold closest?

Meet Wendy

Wendy is passionate about spreading her message and encouraging families to break free of external expectations and instead find the balance in life. She has spoken at numerous conferences and continues to enrich her audiences through ongoing training sessions and seminars where she helps them not only survive, but also thrive.

Having three children of her own, one with special needs, she is constantly redefining what normal looks like in her own family. Wendy has found the real meaning of how a child with special needs can teach you how to live life on your terms and not be trapped by what the  world is expecting of you. As the creator of "Real Families Redefining Normal," she is transforming the way families approach what normal means to them and creating their life, their way.

You can connect more with Wendy at:
www.WendyAndersenPresents.com.

Chapter 12

Don't Read This If You're Perfect
A story of forgiveness

*"You first need to remove the shadow of guilt before
you can truly shine."* – Natasha Botbijl

Let Go

Have you ever wondered what would happen if one day your
entire life was ripped out from under you? If you have, then my
story will resonate with you. It is a story of pain, love, loss and
growth. Perhaps this is your story, too. If you have picked up this
book and landed on this chapter, I hope you keep reading. You are
not here by chance, you are meant to read this. I want to tell you
that you are loved in this place, and you are accepted here no
matter the size and type of baggage you may be carrying in your
heart.

Now, allow me to let you into my world.

It was March 13th, 2010 and I was going to have a beautiful baby boy! I was so excited; our first child, a honeymoon baby. It was a full term, relaxed pregnancy and a beautiful connecting experience —at least that was how it was supposed to go, that was how I had planned it.

Everything started out right.

"Let's get the oil changed today before going to Mom's birthday dinner," I said, feeling pretty active and brave on the day of my due date.

"Sure," was my husband's response to my crazy idea.

What we didn't know was that when our baby started to crown, things would take a turn for the worse and all my plans of a dream life would be lost and thrown into hell.

The moment my baby crowned, a code pink was called (which means a hospital lock-down in the birthing section where all doctors are to report to the room.) He was stuck, and it was too late for a C-section.

They told my family that I may not make it and our son probably wouldn't either, but of course, I do not remember this part. I remember very little after I started to push. I remember feeling helpless, thinking if I just pushed a little harder, I could do this. I remember the silence that followed my last push. I remember SCREAMING at my doctor, asking if my baby was OK. I remember being ignored, thinking that I, somehow, had failed my child.

Then blackness...nothing. I was out, like a candle in a storm.

That moment, I thought I forever lost the things I had spent so long building; the idea of a white picket fence and bright-colored baby clothes disappeared into black space. I lost myself. I failed.

When I woke up, I felt really cold...not in temperature, but rather like I was awake and everything around me was unreal. Like I was watching my life play out through a glass window. I woke up and didn't even ask to see my baby, nor did I even think to ask if he was alive.

I found out later that he was alive, thankfully. However, our pilgrimage was just beginning. We were rushed on to a private plane to the Vancouver Children's Hospital due to complications.

When I saw him in his little air-ready container looking so small, the mother in me burst into tears. I cried and I screamed at myself, blaming myself for failing. I had messed up the one thing I was supposed to be able to do as a woman—bring a healthy child into the world. My child, because of ME, would forever be changed and challenged in life. I blamed myself. I locked myself away, inside. It was my fault. Everything was my fault.

Yet, it wasn't. I wasn't to blame for what happened. In this moment, I was only thinking selfishly about me and about my failure, and that served no one.

It wasn't until later that I realized that when we let go of our need to control everything and perform perfectly, when we lose our reaction to blame, when we embrace life's very flow and allow things to unfold, the universe opens up in an entirely different light.

We are our own worst enemy. We are our own jailer. Often, we get in our own way and create our own prisons. And as much as it seems impossible to break out of, we always have that choice.

I want you to know that you no longer have to hold onto your pain; you can choose freedom, and that choice can happen today.

Forgiveness

When we finally did bring our son home, the time was too short before I had to let him go again.

"I think it's best if you don't stay around the baby alone. I think you need to go to the hospital," my doctor told me. I had severe postpartum depression.

Her words sank me further into my own guilt. I felt worthless. I felt like I had failed again. I felt like giving up. I kept asking myself the wrong questions like, "Why me?"

Yes, I had support and help and people who cared, but as much as they tried to help, they never actually reached ME...the me behind the inner glass wall.

It wasn't until I had no choice but to change that I realized everything I had become was not helping anyone around me, including my spouse, my son and most importantly, myself. My spouse had just been let go from salaried, long-term employment and he was about to embark on his own journey of self-discovery.

What would follow collectively between us is a story meant for another book, a journey of trying times, desperation, humbling moments and deep understanding. Eventually, when I was put up against a wall, I had no other options than to make a choice between allowing the problem to swallow me whole or to break free from it. I started to understand that I could either keep blaming myself and hide, or face the challenges head-on and do the work that needed to be done to find my way out of the despair. Thank goodness for the day I made that discovery.

I chose to find a way out and subsequently move forward.

For me, that meant forgiving myself, understanding that only I can control how I decide to react to what happens around me. I saw life as an ocean, something with no true end and no true beginning, but rather a series of waves I could choose to ride or fight against.

Many times we don't realize that 'fate' is happening around us all the time. We forget that some things must happen to create a bigger picture, and that what seems so big is often so small.

We carry around with us an invisible bag that we use to stuff our hurt, fear, guilt and anger into. As we fill it up, it gets heavier with each new experience, feeling bigger and more powerful until finally we can no longer move without it impacting us and those around us.

We need to empty the bag, and I chose that moment in my life to do so.

I had to release myself from blame and forgive myself. With hindsight, I now see that all of it happened for a reason. At the time, though, it was impossible for me to see that. I understand that releasing myself from my own prison doesn't mean that I will no longer hurt sometimes, but what it does mean is that I can move forward, and that I know I am in control of how often I put my bag down to empty it.

Now it is your turn; what do you need to release to empty your own bag?

Recovery

I turned to neuroscience and neurolinguistic programming to break free from my internal prison. I started to study things on transforming your mind, forgiving yourself, and overcoming your harmful belief systems. In doing so, I became an internationally certified coach (ICF), NLP Practitioner, and a Conversational Intelligence Practitioner (C-IQ).

After finding my way out of my internal maze, filled with many traps and wrong turns, I was able to see that I am enough- as I am- and I can accomplish anything.

I got this, and I can confidentely say you can, too.

Of course, this is a journey. I can still have a bad day and need to use the tools I have learned to remind myself that I am okay the way I am, and I am strong enough to overcome any obstacle in front of me.

I have worked over the years with many women from different countries and some of the things I noticed that we all have in common are as follows:

- We need to forgive either ourselves or someone we know

- We hold onto fears that hold us back

- Our metaprogramming needs constant 'defragging' and 'reframing'

- We truly do create our own fate and reality

I am not saying that this journey is easy, because it's not. I am not telling you it's a straight path, because it's not. I am not even telling you that it will feel like pulling a Band-Aid off, because it won't.

The road to recovery and change is full of your own doubt and fears. It isn't a short journey. It is unique to you. However, I can promise you that should you choose to take action and go down this path, and make changes now, the results are *so* worth it.

I share my story with an open heart in the hopes that it will inspire someone, perhaps you, to understand that regardless of what is happening in your life, you are enough as you are, that you have all that you need within yourself and that no matter what has happened, it is forgivable and inner peace is possible.

You've got this.

I have also put together some special tools and resources just for you. To download these tools and resources visit:

www.yourgrowthmentor.com/womenrising

Meet Natasha

Natasha Botbijl is an Inspirational Speaker, Author, & Success Creator. She works with women going deep into their subconscious and extracting exactly what blocks they may be having, and teaches them how to overcome the barriers and build bridges where the gaps of fear, guilt and uncertainty rest. This is done in a creative and fun way that feels less like deep work and more like an adventure.

On stage, she combines actionable training, authenticity and personal life stories to create a truly powerful experience. Natasha is a straight shooter and says it like it is, which is refreshing; her style is direct, yet supportive.

Her background studies include general psychology from Okanagan College, training at Erickson International as a certified coach (ICF), Neurolinguistic Programing (NLP), Personality Profiling in DISC & Enneagram, and training as a Conversational Intelligence Practitioner (C-IQ), combined with experience in business ownership after having owned multiple award-winning investments.

Throughout the year, she volunteers her time with multiple non-profits such as Vital Voices that helps women in third-world countries start businesses and support their families.

Her ability to help her clients unpack the "gremlins" of self-doubt and make transformations happen all while having fun is unmatched.

When she isn't diving into more training and working with clients, Natasha can be found adventuring around the tropics or with her nose in a book.

Her passion for empowering, guiding and creating change in her clients is surpassed only by her love for her family, which is made up of a special needs son, a daughter, a loving spouse and a small Pomeranian.

You can find out more about Natasha's work or to contact Natasha visit: www.yourgrowthmentor.com.

Chapter 13

The Alchemy of Success
A guide to failing miserably several times (and still winning)

"What if I can be successful by being myself?" - Laura Sprinkle

One of my biggest entrepreneurial failures was a result of deciding not to quit.

I was sitting in the middle of the ocean with my husband on the way back from our honeymoon. I had been offline for over a week, disconnected from my business and "real" life so I could be fully present on our trip.

In the months prior, business had been picking up after I had published a new book, and it was hard to finally put the phone down. I kept thinking about all the things I had not checked off my to-do list yet, but stayed true to my word and stayed out of my inbox.

On the boat, I finally gave in, since the trip was almost over anyway. As I checked emails for the first time in over a week, I saw a sales letter from a friend who was launching something new. I could literally feel her energy coming through the screen; she was that excited. It was obvious how lit up she was with joy, passion and a love for her business.

I burst into tears.

I had disconnected virtually from my business for our trip... but in that moment, I realized I had been disconnected spiritually and emotionally for so much longer.

Jealousy and this aching feeling of "I told you so" started to bubble up within me, as the tears flowed down my face and my bewildered love looked on. I was not jealous of my friend's success, her business or her life. I was jealous because I realized that I had lost the excitement, the joy, the passion and the love for what I was doing long before. I was so stuck in doing the work and going through the motions of creating a successful business that I had lost the connection to myself and what I wanted.

And in that moment, rocking in the waves, I finally decided to quit.

Even though I had the book, the materials, the programs and the website. Even though I had built a community of followers and made money through supporting them.

I had everything that looked like success from the outside, but without the love for my work and a passion for my life, I was stuck in the motions of what looked like flow for others.

I see so many women doing this… going through the motions because they don't know what's next. They don't know where they'll go if they take a different direction.

I knew I had to listen to my intuition. I knew I had to follow the guidance that was so clearly put in front of me. My fire had gone out long ago, but with the realization and that decision to do something about it, I was set alight.

I had no idea what I was doing, but passion and excitement led me to delete my entire business. The Soul Fire Revolution was born with that new spark inside of me and, starting from scratch, I tripled my following and income within two months. Seriously, tripled what it had taken me two years to do previously.

Every month, it grew bigger and bigger. Over and over and over I poured gasoline on the flames, sparking more passion and bigger successes. I was giving it all that I had, and I felt like I was on top of the world with each launch doing better than the last. The wins just kept on coming.

That is, until I found myself completely burnt out. And I thought, "What. The. Hell. How did I get back here?"

I thought I had figured out the answer, that the fire and passion was lacking from my business. I had made the changes and became wildly successful beyond what I had imagined was possible, but the light and the flame had overtaken my life.

I was left with no air and no space to breathe, all of my light went out and I was left in darkness once more.

This failure was different, though, because I knew what the passion and fire felt like. I could feel the void now more clearly than ever, and in that darkness with nothing left to give, I sunk into a depression.

There was no money coming in, and all my contact with the outside world came to a crashing halt. As the wins turned into hits, it felt like every step I took zapped all my waning energy... and all those steps seemed to be going in the wrong direction. I was so embarrassed that everything had fizzled out and turned to dust.

In that space, I started to question again, "Why?!" I had been so fired up and I still felt the love and joy and passion for my work... but it was muted. It was silent.

One day, after a couple of months, it got to the point where I wasn't going to be able to make rent. I sat with my husband in the Portland Public Library and looked at him so full of shame, so full of disappointment in myself and so full of despair that I felt like I was on the brink of insanity.

I did the only thing I could think to do; I took out my pen and I made a list of five things I could do to make money and pay my rent. The first thing on the list, by intuitive design apparently, was to reach out via text to five friends to ask for help.

Sending those messages felt like coming out of the ashes and breathing air into my business once more. Not knowing what would come of it, but at the same time knowing that everything was about to change.

Instead of passing me a contact number for the local Starbucks, which I would have gladly accepted, they asked me to support them in their businesses.

I thought that seemed kind of crazy. Did they know that I was such a huge loser that I couldn't even make rent? Did they know that my last launch hadn't garnered even a peep from my tribe?

I mulled it over in the best way I know how: a really long walk. A couple of hours in, I was heading past the ocean when it hit me like a wave.

Everything had been a natural pattern. Each moment of my journey had been made up of elements that either worked together in synergy or caused another to crash. Earth, water, air and fire were all needed in creating sustainable success in my business, just like they're all needed in creating the workings of everything in the Universe. What I learned was that when I was overly focused on only one element of my life, whether it was totally rooted in creating the foundational pieces of my work, or only focused on content for content's sake, or all lit up with passion and joy...

Everything fell apart.

When I asked for help in that library, it allowed me to bring air into my fiery business. As I walked by the water, I realized I also needed more flow and consistency.

The realization that this could help bring both my business and my life into balance was incredible. It was like those moments of disaster had turned into gifts that I could use to help not only myself, but more people all over the world as well.

Earth - In order to rise, you must grow your roots deep and strong.

The grounding elements in your business are intuitively obvious once you recognize them. They're the foundation of your work and often where most people begin. Who do you serve, what do you do, what products do you sell - these are the foundational questions whose answers become the soil from which your business grows.

The Earth element activities should not just be something you do at the beginning of your entrepreneurial journey. Often when you're feeling overwhelmed, it's because you need to go back to basics and create foundational systems that serve both you and your customers more effectively.

We cannot rise without time spent putting down entrepreneurial roots. Some extremely important and grounding technique are connecting with your tribe on a deeper level, investing in technologies to support you and working on your business rather than in it. If you're feeling pulled in all directions, try rooting down for a while.

As vital as Earth is, many of my clients feel stuck and like they can't move forward because their foundation isn't yet solid. They're spending way too much time on creating their websites, tweaking their logos and investing in programs that teach them the basics of creating a business. In this case, they're way too rooted in the Earth element and need to breathe life back into their businesses. If this is you, it's time to move into one of the other elements.

Water - In order to move ahead, you must create flow with consistency.

The element of Water is all about the flow in your business - it's fed by using consistency in your marketing, through your conversations with your tribe, and in the flow of income. Whether that means sending weekly newsletters, creating a powerful morning routine or sticking to a social media schedule, all of these things ensure that the tap is consistently running and new customers are constantly being created.

While Water can bring so much good to a business, staying in the water element can make it feel like you're drowning in your to-do lists. This often happens when you get a flood of new customers or clients, or when you've hit capacity on your systems - there's no more riverbank (Earth) to contain the flow of water and it spills over.

In order for water to flow smoothly, it requires the Earth below and beside it as well as space and Air to move and breath. One of my clients came to me and thought she was totally rocking her Water, but when I took a look at her schedule, it was clear that there was something wrong.

It was FULL. Every single minute, of every single day, from wake to sleep.

Fires happen. Winds blow. Boulders spring up out of nowhere. If you're so in the flow that you can't pivot when necessary, it's going to feel like everything comes crashing down, like a wave over a carefully built sandcastle Jenga set, when something goes awry.

I'm sure you've probably had one of those days... where everything has to work in alignment or it will all fail. You have five meetings, a lunch date, a doctor's appointment and a big project due. You've got it all in your calendar, including travel time, just so. And that's the day that something happens. Leave room for Water to flow and this won't be a problem.

Air - In order to grow you must spread the word about your business.

When I was stuck in my depression and feeling stagnant in my business, I was able to breathe life back into it through the element of Air. By reaching out to my network and asking for support, I opened up the winds of change.

You can do this, too, by attending networking events, asking friends to become affiliates to spread the word about your launches, and talking about what you do in a meaningful way.

This is often the step my clients fear most. I can get them to make tweaks to their web copy with no complaints, but the minute I ask them to interview potential customers, they seize up. The thing is, you don't need to have gale-force winds in order to get people talking about your business. A small breeze can make a huge difference, and even talking to one person about what you do can change everything.

When the wind is blowing in your direction, you feel on top of the world in business... sort of like when you're on a sailboat at sunset in the Tropics. Although I haven't experienced that, I still know that it would feel similarly to having throngs of people clamoring to work with me and pay me tons of money. Okay, maybe not exactly the same, but you get what I mean.

When Air is out of balance -- well, that's when your life can start to blow up. It could feel like a hurricane - smashing through all of your well thought out plans. Maybe it feels like you're blowing in the wind, directionless. If you're the kind of person that goes where the wind takes you, then you might want to be careful of staying too long in this element. This is when getting some Earth under your feet or creating consistency with Water would help to channel your Air in right direction.

Fire - In order to attract your tribe, you must use your own passionate spark.

Passion and fire for your business are often what's viewed as the sexy marketing in business - and for good reason; it works. Passion attracts passion. It's really easy to burn out, however, if we're always here, always full-force with our energy and never pausing to rest. Often, we're told to delegate all but what lights us up - everything but the fire. This is also why CEOs get burnt out. They need some of the foundational tasks of the Earth, some of the consistency of Water and some of the networking of Air to keep them sane.

On the other side, many of my clients ignore their inner spark and their inner desire for something more. Your spark is like the special sauce that you bring to the table in your business. Lighting it up attracts your tribe to you - like everyone coming together around a campfire. Ignoring it means you stifle your own inner soul-fire.

I was talking with a client who was coming up with some ideas around her wellness business. She kept mentioning things like balance, yoga, inner peace... the same old words you'd align with any wellness business. She wasn't passionate about it and you could tell she was even boring herself.

Then she said to me, "What I really want to talk about is..." My ears perked up and I was hooked with that sentence alone. Your inner desires are contagious and can catch like wildfire.

"What I really want to talk about is hot mama, leather-wearing, motorcycle-riding badass women who rock their sexiness."

Well, hot damn! I don't even like motorcycles but I'd much rather be in that tribe than the balance and inner peace one. Her fire was potent in that moment and so much more magnetic than trying to be like everyone else. Use your inner spark and your business will be the same way.

Most importantly, long-term success requires an understanding that no part of your life exists in isolation and that you must care for your whole self to truly flourish.

Nowadays, I bring in all the elements for my clients so that no one needs to burn, rust, drown, or decay unnecessarily. I show them that they actually can have success in the short term, sustainable growth in the long term and shine their light as brightly as possible without getting run down.

That being said, if you do find yourself in any of those situations - right now or in the future - no need to worry. Nature always knows best, and sometimes the most tremendous growth happens right after a forest fire, a hurricane, a mudslide or a flood. Take a deep breath, rest where needed and continue in the best way you know how.

The good news is using these elemental practices as a guide will allow you to experience that tremendous growth with fewer and fewer catastrophes, as you'll inherently become more connected to what the Universe wants for you. Hint: The Universe wants for you the same things you want for yourself. This practice makes it that much easier to come into it with ease.

Rise Up Challenges

Water - If you're feeling like you're drowning in your to-do list, write out everything you have to do on a piece of paper. Then label each item: For now, for later, for never, for someone else.

Fire - If you're feeling burnt out, step back and ground. Take a week or a day or even an hour and just breath and connect with your feet on the ground.

Air - If you're feeling like you're moving with no direction, channel that flow into consistency by sticking to one activity per day.

Earth - If you're feeling stagnant and stuck, reach out to a few friends. Dance and move the energy around.

Meet Laura

Laura Sprinkle is a creative launch and brand strategist who combines intuition and sales funnels to support soulful entrepreneurs in growing their businesses naturally. The creator of Empire Alchemy™, she uses the elements to guide business owners into their desires with more ease and fun.

She has run business growth workshops for her tribe of thousands for several years, been honored to share her story in dozens of speaking engagements, podcasts & interviews and loves to sit down over a cappuccino and talk strategy and soul.

Laura knows the difference between outward success and deep, heart-centered satisfaction in business because she's experienced them both and can intuitively guide you toward your passion and purpose while making the money and impact you're meant to. Her favorite things include helping business owners launch for profit in an authentic way, cute coffee shops and autumn leaves.

Find out how to create your own alchemical empire at www.laurasprinkle.com.

Chapter 14

A Positive Attitude Can Create A Beautiful Life
How mindset, self-care and ambition can lead to joyful living

"Visualizing your big picture can be empowering... especially when you surround yourself with people who want you to get there!"
- Sarah Shakespeare

I have always been a happy person. I loved people and loved to socialize. As a child, I was that little girl who "Lit up the room." I felt embraced wherever I went.

Raised in England by a Jamaican father and an English mother, I was part of a fun-loving family. I didn't have much as a child - we lived in the poorest area of town in a small house, and I felt lucky to have what I had. I was told often from my parents that I was very special little girl.

My brother was born 11 months before me, so we were raised like twins. My sister was born when I was 11 yrs. old. I felt excited to have a new baby in the house, and finally I had a sister! I always helped my mother with the new baby, but continued to receive a lot of attention from my parents and maintain a close relationship with my brother.

My father was a popular man and I felt like a "Daddy's girl" right from the beginning. He constantly told me that I could achieve anything that I put my mind to. He was so proud to be a Jamaican living in England and wanted his children to live a wonderful life. He taught me that manners and respect were important and that there were no excuses for bad manners!

Education was important to my father as well, and I was reminded regularly how amazing it was for me to have an education. In Jamaica, education was seen as a privilege. My future was important to my father, and he supported me in every area of my education. I lived in a home with rules: there was no television until homework was done!

I was into sports in school, particularly sprinting. I won many races during my teenage years. I pushed hard to be successful, visualizing winning each race before I ran it. Of course, the pressure was on at home from my Dad to bring home Gold!

I did the best I could. I won the Girls 100m Sprint every year in High School and always ran the last leg of the 4 x100m Relay because I knew that I could bring it home for the team. We won every year.

When I started High School, I attended a school that was out of my catchment area. It had a great reputation and my father was excited when I was allowed to attend there. This new school was a forty-five minute bike ride from my house or, if I walked, a 90-minute commute. I never complained. I knew I had been given a great opportunity to attend this school and felt grateful for the opportunity.

Attending outside of my catchment meant that I would go through the rest of my school years attending a different school than my neighbors. However, I was excited to met new people and felt confident that I would make new friends. I would smile and chat with people on my way to and from school; my love for people became apparent as I grew older and more independent.

My school was in a rich area of town and I would walk and bike past many fine homes and beautiful properties along the way. It made me think about how people lived differently as I had lived my whole life, in the poorest part of town. While walking to school, I would visualize my future to include a fine home and a fancy garden.

Although I had a happy home and a great childhood full of many laughs, I still wanted more out of life. I would think about what it would take for me to get there. It wasn't really money that motivated me because I had never had any, but I knew that it would take hard work AND money to get what I wanted in life. It was around this age that I started to think about my "Big Picture" and how I wanted my future to look.

When I was 15-years-old, I got my first job working at a Florist. I loved it, and immediately was given substantial responsibility from my bosses. I felt proud that I was trusted to assume these duties at such a young age. It made me see that working hard could be enjoyable if you found something that you loved. I was excited to earn my own money and was given the freedom to spend it as I liked- I believe that is when I started to enjoy retail therapy!

As I started Grade 12, I became even more sociable and had amazing nights out with my friends. It was around that age that I started to pay attention to my physical appearance. I was overweight, but because I still performed well in my sports teams, I did not notice the extra weight creeping on. I was strong and fit and could run fast, so that's all that had mattered. My mother was an amazing cook, so it was like having a personal chef cook your favourite meals. I had not even heard of counting calories.

I had been saving some money from my job and decided I wanted some new clothes for my ever-expanding social life. It was a miserable shopping trip as I discovered that nothing fit me. I went into a fashionable teen store and it became apparent that "plus size" was the only way to go. I was very disappointed, and ended my shopping trip abruptly because I was so upset. I left the mall with my money in my purse and a new resolve to take action towards improving my health.

I decided to join fitness classes in addition to riding my bicycle everywhere. I joined Weight Watchers and lost 35 pounds. I focused on my health and was excited when I was able to buy clothes that I loved. I started to realize that if I focused on something that was important to me, I could be successful at whatever I wanted. I didn't let anything or anyone deter me from achieving my weight loss goal. This one decision was instrumental in me learning the importance of self-care, and I realized that it was important that I felt and looked healthy.

When I was 16, I met my first serious boyfriend. As I write this, we are sharing our 27th year together and we have been blessed with three beautiful daughters. My husband told me that the first thing he noticed about me was my smile and positive attitude. Our relationship moved quickly; I knew he was destined to be my life partner. We moved into our first place together after seven weeks and never looked back. Our first pregnancy was planned and our first daughter was born when I was 18 yrs. old.

I was excited to start my family with a man that had the same life vision as I. Although we had distinct personalities, we also had the same life goals. I was the life and soul of the party where he was quiet. I followed my intuition and knew that this was the start of the "Big Picture" that I had visualized.

When my daughter was five weeks old, I decided to join the Gym. It turned out to be one of the best decisions that I would ever make. It took me about two weeks to decide that fitness would be the career for me.

I got great results from my workouts. I had an elevated mood and I had a body that I loved. With 65 lbs. to lose after my pregnancy, I went back to Weight Watchers to focus once again on my nutrition. I managed to lose the weight and maintained it until my next pregnancy, 10 years later.

At 18, I also I decided to live an alcohol free life. I knew that alcohol would set me back in life and impact my health in a negative way. I saw it as a waste of money and didn't want to have headaches and wasted days after a Girl's Night Out. I saw many people around me struggling with alcoholism and decided that there would be no space made in my day for any of the drama that accompanied it.

By 19, I was a Personal Trainer. I loved my job and felt blessed to have a job that made me feel like I was socializing all day at work. I enjoyed the gym atmosphere and spent 12 hours a day there!

As my popularity as a trainer grew, so did my income, to the point that it far exceeded my expectations. It seemed surreal to me that I could both be rewarded financially for making a positive impact on others, and help people meet their fitness goals. I knew that I had found my career.

While I spent my time at the gym, my husband's business continued to grow. We were blessed in that we had family nearby to help with our daughter. We were starting to see the results of our hard work and dedication and felt motivated every day to continue towards our Big Picture.

My gratitude for life started to show in every area of my life. I was happy and those visions from my teenage years were coming together nicely.

At 26, we moved from England to Canada. While I loved my life in England, my instincts told me that the move would be a great opportunity. My positive attitude and optimistic outlook helped me to adjust to the move. I had two more children once we moved, but I made sure that I did not lose focus on my own health and wellbeing. I worked out through both pregnancies and took care to look my best.

With three daughters to raise, I worked part-time as a personal trainer while my husband focused on building his construction business. We moved forward with our life plan.

We have built and renovated many beautiful homes. This gave me an opportunity to use my love of interior design as we made the homes show-home ready. Even today, this continues to be a passion of mine. As I look at my beautiful backyard with amazing views in the background, it takes me back to my school day commutes and the visions I held for my own future, walking past those fine homes and gardens in the prestigious neighborhoods along my route. I realize that without a doubt, I have created this beautiful life for my family and myself.

As I look back over my life, I realize that I have learned several things about happiness moving through my young life.

Your Mindset Leads to Action

I realized at a young age that I often looked at things differently than other people. My positive outlook allowed me to send positive energy towards people. I helped to lift them up when they weren't feeling good. I like to look at the most positive outcome first and see how that would feel if that was the reality of the situation. I believe that mindset leads to action and creates your reality.

You need to realize that great things don't happen overnight. Set goals in place so that you know where you are going. You can't have an amazing life while sitting down and thinking about it- you have to have an action plan!

Self Care - Give Yourself Time

Self–care in any form, be it a daily workout, meditation, drinking tea with friend or having a pedicure is essential. When you are energized and satisfied with your life then you're able to give back to others. Make a weekly plan to take time for yourself to do things that make you feel happy. When your mood is lifted it can increase your positive outlook on life. It may only be 10 minutes a day, but remember it's your time and you are worth it.

Ambition and Inner Drive

Do you have an inner drive that you are hiding inside because you're afraid of the reactions of others? What are you doing to excel everyday? I believe that it is never too late to live your desired life. Why not look on the bright side of life? You can truly think of yourself as great. Regardless of your life circumstances, anything can be overcome. Think about your bigger picture and visualize what that means to you. Your idea of a successful life is likely to be a different from others...define what success means to you.

Rise Up Challenge

We are lucky to be alive. This thing called LIFE is a gift. It is important to our success that we have gratitude for the life we have been given. Take some time and think about what you are grateful for. The list is probably longer than you think. Once you identify what amazing things are present in your life, you will begin to feel a shift in your mindset. Try not to lose sight of the fact that something you complain about may very well be someone else's dream life.

Write down your short and long-term goals. Add a timeline if needed so that you can stay focused on the plan. It may take one month, one year or even five years to get where you want to be, but be realistic about what you're trying to achieve and focus on your big picture.

Look at what or who creates negativity in your life. Make strides to avoid negative situations, as they will not help you create a positive mindset. Surround yourself with people who believe in you.

Self-care is critical to your wellbeing, so take an honest look at how you are treating yourself. Look at your week and prioritize what has to be done. Make it a priority to set aside some time for you every day. You will be surprised at how good you feel afterwards. You may feel guilty at first, but you have to realize that if you're not "full of yourself," you can't give back to others. Make good choices regarding your health and when you feel good, look good and feel energized, your life will be amazing for you and everyone around you!

Meet Sarah

Sarah Shakespeare is a lover of life and wishes to live 'till 100 years old. Many of her friends and family know that she's on the "100-year plan!"

As a Personal Trainer/Coach for nearly 25 years, she loves to help people improve their lives through creating a healthy lifestyle that enriches all areas of their life.

Her love of exercise has led her to complete many Marathons, Ultra-Marathons and compete in and win fitness competitions. She gained her pro card in fitness in 2006 at The World Championships.

As someone who is very goal-driven, she has come to know that success really comes from first sculpting a positive mind, and she loves to pass her positive energy onto others. She believes that in order to live a happy, successful life you have to have a positive mindset and this is one of the key skills she helps her clients master.

Sarah is a wife, mother of three daughters and a good friend to many. She is friendly, loves to laugh and has a "Glass is Full" attitude about life, which is very contagious.

A dream come true was when she moved from England to Canada in 2000, calling it her "Millennium Move" after visiting Canada nine times on holiday! It has been a decision that she has never regretted and calls herself "An English Girl in Canada" who loves the Summer more than the Winter!

Her ultimate desire is to help others create their own life plan, and achieve their life goals through healthy living, a positive mindset and having the support and accountability to make them happen.

As an energetic leader she always leads by example and has lived many of her dreams already from building several homes, moving to Canada, travelling around the world, competing and winning competitions and living life to the fullest every year as she continues with her 100 year plan!

You can find out how to create your dream life plan at www.sarahshakespeare.com.

Chapter 15

Coming Home
What legacy will you leave?

"Each breath of life is a mystery. It marks both the beginning of our existence and the end of our life." - Marjorie Miller

My thoughts were racing.

A lingering feeling of urgency, my jaw tightening and the painful wave of emotion washed over me as I tried to focus on pleasing the people at that party. I was 17-years-old and finally dating my kindergarten crush. That night, I was stressed and my insecurity manifested in an endless spiral of emotions as I was meeting his family for the first time. My face was flushed red, serving as a tormenting reminder that I must keep it together. I wanted to be the perfect girl. I wanted his family, who I didn't know well at all, to approve of and like me.

Then it happened...

Some of the details are burned in my mind, and I remember clearly smiling while keeping up with the performance. My boyfriend was standing right next to me as I looked down at my feet, gathering my thoughts and trying with all my might to swallow a piece of potato without making too much noise.

But something was wrong.

After a couple seconds without any results, I decided to ask for water. My eyes widened as I tried to vocalize the words, only to realize that I lost the ability to speak and I couldn't breathe.

I was so busy performing.

I was so busy trying to act like nothing was wrong.

I ignored all the warning signs and I was on the verge of a big wake up call.

Feeling I didn't have control pushed me into panic. A sudden feeling of dread, my sweaty hands, the pounding of my heart, the dizziness, the unsteady twisting of my body into terror... the whole room seeming to shrink while everybody stared at me.

I slowly drifted away and all of a sudden... peace. I felt this incredible feeling of love as flashes and memories of my life came rushing towards me. The sweetness of my mom's voice while I was growing in her tummy, her soft touch, her love. My grandfather smiling at me and holding me tight and my grandmother's unconditional love. My dad's generosity and loving words. My sister's love, always there with me. Those long walks in the valley conversing for hours with God. I was surrounded by emotions, deep soul-stirring feelings. I felt loved. I felt happy. I could have stayed there forever embraced in this tranquil beauty, but the spell was suddenly broken by an immense force. Suddenly, I was back at the moment, a big piece of potato flying out of my mouth like an angry bullet.

Each breath of life is a mystery.

It marks the beginning of our existence and it marks the end of life. Breathing occurs 20 to 25 thousand times each day without us even thinking about it. When we are deprived of even one breath, our body screams and struggles.

You might not ever find yourself in this kind of situation.

But then again, how often have you felt suffocated in your life?

How often have you silenced yourself and gotten disconnected from what is truly important, allowing all the insecurities to form a tight grip on your throat?

Twenty years later, here I sit on the floor, feeling the pain and the powerlessness of losing an old friend. We had so many beautiful memories together - our first Kindergarten class, the matching tattoos we got together in Junior High while hiding from the Nuns during a sleepover retreat, her smile and her loving spirit. I can't stop myself from smiling even as I cry because she lived her life fully, and I know that even if she didn't have time to say goodbye to her little babies, they knew their Mamá loved them and lived her life without any regrets.

When I had choked at that party twenty years past, the memories played out before me so peacefully. I wonder what it will look like the next time I take my last breath. Will it be peaceful with beautiful, loving images of my children, husband, family and friends just like it was when I was 17?

Or is it going to be scary and painful because I failed to truly appreciate what matters the most?

The first half of my life, I was full of wonder and love for life and everyone around me. Against my Mom's lamentations, I couldn't help but bring stray dogs to my home or go visit my handful of old grandmothers in the "house of the forgotten" where they were left to die in the last bit of their lives.

Every Sunday, I would wake up early and walk to the small church in my town to teach Sunday School. Twice a week during my junior year, together with some friends, we visited the Maria Droste Center where I learned from a group of incredible women all about resilience and how they fought every day to improve their lives in the face of physical suffering, abuse and humiliation.

María was my friend there. Her eyes were dark, her hands small and her body showed the stress of childbearing and abuse. Her expression was withdrawn at times, her voice was shy and her words were sad. We spent most afternoons learning the alphabet while my friends watched her kids. Tears often formed in her eyes as she learned, at age 37, to write her name for the very first time. She never stopped coming to see me, never missed a day of her lessons.

I was also very close to my inner voice. I call it God, some people call it intuition or the universe. I had really engaging, nourishing conversations with God at nighttime before going to sleep, during my long walks in the valley, while climbing trees or simply while I was sitting on the bus going home. I heard the wisdom and I felt the love in the words and, most importantly, I trusted the voice and without any doubt, followed it.

Serving God and Loving were my North Stars during the early part of my life. Yes, I had a unique upbringing. I grew up in a small pueblo in Ecuador. In this little village, I lived in a home that was a part of a compound of five homes. This compound was made up of aunts, uncles, cousins, grandmothers and more. Together, we formed a community made from family and LOVE where Happiness was Home made every day.

The second half of my life, I did the opposite. First, I stopped talking to God. Somehow, I got scared of God. Perhaps it was his power, perhaps it was the fear of dying of cancer. I grew increasingly angry and resentful with God as what was supposed to be an easy, short battle turned into me spending the better part of my teens, twenties and early thirties at war with my body. It was years of surgeries, radiation treatments and countless appointments with doctors and specialists at clinics and hospitals. It was exhausting, to say the least. Perhaps it was my yearning to fit in a new culture and to belong. Perhaps it was the business that sucked me into a new life where my weeks, months and years became an endless pressure to perform, to keep up and to survive between all the setbacks, diapers, sport practices, piano lessons, ear infections, bills, food shopping and a hundred other things life throws at you.

Just as you cannot sustain a body without food, you cannot sustain a spirit without God. With heaviness in my heart, I see how that happy and authentic girl faded little by little as I let all my insecurities tighten the grip on my throat. The overwhelming feeling of shame gave me the urgency to take up less space and to hide. I didn't want to stand out, so I played small. I went with the flow instead of singing my own song and speaking up.

It gives me the chills to think about that part of my life, mostly because I think that my daughters would have been the ones that lost the most by not having their mother sharing what brought happiness, carcajadas (loud laughs), and joy to their lives. And because I know that if I were to die before "coming back home," the last minutes of my life would feel like a struggle and my flashbacks would be full of regret.

I believe that the combination of flashbacks is your legacy. And as we all approach that time, living one day closer to our last, I can't emphasize enough the importance of living true to you and living authentically. Know that you are the Queen, the King, the Princess or the Goddess who has full control in how you decide to walk the path of your life. Know that you are here with a purpose and you are here to take on this beautiful world full of possibilities and abundance. It is your life and you are responsible for it, so start now. Take ownership of your own life and one by one, own your feelings, your scars, your fear, your strength and your power.

Own Your Feelings: Don't ever shut down your feelings, instead run towards them so you can explore their beauty.

Own Your Scars: Celebrate the scars you have been accumulating along the way; share them with others as it will create a domino healing effect.

Own Your Fear: Your fear is your close friend who shows up in your life right at the instant when you are about to grow a bigger crown.

Own Your Strength: Don't accept the default of your life and challenge the status quo, as there are always new ways to bring more love and beauty to this world.

Own Your Power: Accept nothing less than the breathtaking truth that you are never alone, and that you are capable of miracles by letting the voice of God guide you.

Finally, in my home, the common thread is Love. Put those words together, Home and Love, and you get HomeLove. HomeLove represents a pathway of authenticity; practice and baby steps that help me navigate the constant transformation and reshaping of the world. Home to me is the full voice and power of my soul, all those quirky, peculiar and inimitable things that make me unique and full of life.

I believe completely that life is not about avoiding death, but is all about deciding with every experience to "come home."

"Coming home" has changed my relationship with my children. It has helped me pass on the joy of service, my love for nature and my close relationship with God. It makes me happy to know that one day, when I am not here, they will take my wisdom and pass it on to a new generation in a new world I can't even begin to imagine.

Today, there are still times of chaos and sadness in my life, but I embrace them instead of pretending they are not there. As I embrace them one by one, I can see how my spirit emerges wiser, stronger and more complete.

How about you? Are you ready to Come Home?

Rise-Up Challenge
Start the Fire and Keep It Alive

First, let me ask you this- have you ever built a fire? What do you need to build a fire? You need a bundle of wood, tinder and kindling. Then you place your tinder and kindling in the middle of your campfire and stack the wood, making sure there is enough air circulating in between the logs. Then you light it from below. Voila, you've got a beautiful fire! Here is the trick; to keep the fire alive, you need to keep feeding it more wood. Right?

Now, think about that fire- that fire represents your soul waiting to awaken and once awake you MUST keep feeding its flame otherwise the fire might weaken and extinguish.

To awaken the soul and keep its flame alive, you need to nurture it. You nurture your soul the way you nurture a newborn; with time and love. If your soul has been weakened for too long, then know there is going to be resistance. So start slow! Start by committing to a daily date with yourself where you spend time reflecting and releasing. You reflect when there is stillness, silence and solitude- a hot bath before going to sleep, a short walk in the woods, journaling or simply by closing your eyes. During this quiet time, keep it simple and think only about your blessings. You release when you move your body- it is an instant therapy that will leave you peaceful, but with increased energy. Pick something you like to do- my favorite is dancing and running.

Coming home is a journey and you must *Start the Fire and Keep It Alive.* The power of nurturing your soul will bring you more clarity, greater emotional stability, balance, wisdom and help you become closer to the *blueprint of your home.* Commit! You cannot afford not to find the time to fulfill the legacy for which you were created, as it will not only mean regret in your last breath, but it represents a loss for your children, your partner, your family, your friends and the world.

Meet Marjorie

Marjorie Miller is a Bilingual English/Spanish Inspirational Speaker, Author, & Business Start-Up Coach, addressing audiences around the world.

Her background studies include a B.A in Business Administration & Marketing in addition to Integrative Health, Quantum and Transformational Coaching Certifications combined with a 10+ year entrepreneurship career in both online and brick and mortar businesses.

She is the founder of The HomeLove Movement, a safe haven for moms filled with powerful, courageous and honest stories written by legendary moms who have witnessed and conquered many obstacles in their lives.

In her business coaching practice, she works with passionate and independent moms in the early stages of starting a business. She helps her clients go from conceptual ideas to paying clients by envisioning, branding and crafting their unique strategies with ease and flow and a competitive edge.

She is also the creator of Moms On a Mission Journey where she guides mothers around the world to leave a legacy of authenticity and love. She inspires moms to make a positive impact in the world by gathering their courage to break the status quo and to fully show up in the way they love, parent and live.

Born and raised in a small pueblo in Ecuador, she loves to get her hands dirty by working in her garden growing her own vegetables. Marjorie also loves to volunteer, dance, run, travel, savor new foods and read anything she can get her hands on- especially if it's about business or personal development.

Marjorie lives in Seattle, Washington with her husband Jacob raising two active young girls, Solé and Tessa.

If you are ready to connect with other moms on a mission to create businesses that make a positive impact in the world and who want to raise the next generation of well-balanced, peaceful, and mindful leaders join them here: http://thehomelovemovement.com/.

Chapter 16

True Abundance
Live a life of freedom now

"Abundance is not a final destination. It is how we live our life everyday." - Maria Conde

Everyone is worthy of true abundance, but what that looks like for each person is different. Living a life of true abundance is more than just the bottom line of your financials. It is about how you show up and live your life.

My journey with money began at an early age as I watched from my bedroom window over the driveway as the bank took our family vehicle away. My parents had declared bankruptcy. I did not fully understand what all the commotion was about, but I was able to sense the anger and shame at that moment. At the tender age of eight, I acquired the belief that image was not only a critical part of who you were, but it could also make you someone special and important. Those feelings of being special and being accepted was somewhat of a challenge for me, as I was born to a Caucasian mother and a Black father. At the time I was growing up, racism was rampant in the States. I desperately yearned for love and acceptance outside our family home. I watched as my parents did the "Keeping up with the Jones'" routine and buried themselves further in debt.

Significant amounts of money entered my life for the first time at the age of 13, working as a nanny for a prominent family. At the age of 19, I got my first credit card while finishing college, which in itself made me feel special. After college, I went on to become a professional accountant. I had excellent jobs and successfully managed large groups of accountants. At 38, I was divorced and had not had any children, yet it was something I felt was really important for me to do. With my biological clock ticking, I did not want to wait until I found the right partner, so I took the necessary steps through my local fertility clinic to have a child on my own. Again, people always told me how amazed they were at my strength and accomplishments. In life, if I want something, I go after it and I get it.

This is the happy side of my story. That doesn't mean there wasn't a dark side, though.

Even though I was strong, amazing and accomplished, I had a serious problem lurking in the background: debt. With this debt came huge amounts of crippling SHAME. After all, I was a money professional. I knew better. This fact was rubbed in my face more than once by loved ones. Every time I heard this, my self-worth would sink further down. I was just as hard on myself, as I could successfully manage millions of dollars of other peoples' money but could not manage my own paycheck.

Although I made large amounts of money from an early age, I seemed unable to do the right things with it. What I did learn from that young age was that spending money made me feel good, especially on others. I would buy gifts to gain love and acceptance from family and friends.

Take a moment to think who is on your gift list, and why you choose to buy for them. Often, we buy gifts for people when we feel guilty about not spending time with them or we do it to buy their affection.

Acceptance has always been important for me. I often longed to be "part of the group." Like everyone, I am a unique individual. I like to live life on my terms, and having this freedom is very important to me. Because of this, I may make decisions that are not consistent with the mainstream population. I have accepted this now, but for a good part of my life I had not. I had a low self-worth, low self-esteem and I used money to make myself feel good. I lived for my credit cards.

Every month as I reviewed my bills, I would feel that sense of overwhelming shame. While I was not in denial about my debt, I did not want to do anything about that dark cloud. I was not willing to give up the feeling of power and approval it gave me. Even with large amounts of debt, I somehow managed to never miss a payment or have a collection call, and I was able to maintain a decent credit score. I had to, in order to guarantee I could always get more of that drug-like money.

Even after I worked through my challenges and became more successful, I could not come out with my whole story because of the shame that plagued me. I also recognized that not sharing my story was not serving anyone, so I became a money coach to help people who were just like me. I felt like I was qualified on a personal level because I knew what my clients were feeling, the excuses they would make to allow themselves to spend and the stories they would tell themselves to make it all okay. I knew all about the world of denial they lived in and often why they denied the true reality of their situation.

Many of us have what I call the Monkey Money Mind! This little monkey tells us the stories that our subconscious mind believes and lives out. Although I'm talking about debt and spending here, this is also true for those who are under-earners. Many people are afraid to charge what they are worth. They are afraid their clients will not pay higher prices or that they will lose them. Many people are also uncomfortable having significant amounts of money in their possession, and this prevents them from being financially successful. Working through those blocks is essential to living your life in true abundance. We often don't realize what we already have and the abundance that we currently have in our lives.

When looking back, my journey has included three big lessons that have moved me forward, changed my money legacy and allowed me to release the shame.

Your Why

A major turning point in my life came when I lost one of my dearest friends and my own life coach. Even though I have experienced many deaths in my lifetime, including both my parents, none compared to the grief I felt from her death. Her celebration of life was one of the most gut-wrenching yet life-altering moments in my life.

I sat on the edge of my seat in the church, sobbing, tears rolling down my face. As I watched her life play on the screen above me,

I was moved to see her impact on this world. She had lived such a full and beautiful life. As I sat there, a feeling of hollowness crept over me. 'What was I doing with my life?'

In that moment, her death and her legacy became my catalyst for change. I knew that it was my pile of debt that was holding me back from the change I so desperately craved.

Once I discovered my 'why' in life, it propelled me in the right direction to take the necessary actions, putting me on the path I desired.

My 'why' is for all women to rise to their fullest potential. The world needs them. The world needs you and your gifts. Their upper limits, self-sabotaging behaviors and lack of vision can prevent this from happening. This is why I am here today, writing to you. Knowing your true 'why' can propel you, too. Discovering your true 'why', however, is not that simple. Begin by asking yourself the simple question of "what do I truly want?" Then ask yourself this again, at least two more times. Dive deep for the answers. Your first round will most likely be on the surface level. Go deeper to find your true 'why' and it will propel you to where you want to go. Holding this vision gave me the fuel to get through the tough stuff and guided me on my path.

Your Mindset

Over the years, I tried several things to help me get out of debt. I've tracked every penny, kept my credit cards frozen in ice and read dozens of books on money management, which I studied for years professionally. Some of these books I read more than once, but not once did I internalize them. Over the years I made gradual progress, but nothing as significant as I had wanted to, until one day I picked up a new book at the bookstore. Actually, I believe the book found me; as soon as I started reading it I finally understood why I had behaved the way I did with money. It was like a beautiful sunrise after a long stretch of dark, rainy days. All of a sudden I felt ok with my money. I felt the constant pressure of the debt release. It is not important which specific book it was as the teacher will arrive when the student is ready. And I was ready. That book was my teacher, so perhaps this book will be yours?

That life-changing book I had stumbled upon was about mindset. You see, all of our money issues are anchored to the stories we have formed about money as we have moved throughout our lives. I learned that I could change my mindset and control my Monkey Money Mind. For the control freak that I am, this was a great win! The awareness I have now is strong enough to know when I am triggered and how to tame my Monkey Money Mind. The Monkey Money Mind never totally goes away, you just learned to co-exist with it in a much healthier way. With a new mindset and the right tools, I learned how to have true abundance in my life. This allowed me to let go of all my shame surrounding my debt and finances, discover the abundance that already existed in my life and to have gratitude for it all. You can have this too.

For me, I had two big, primary mindsets that had to change. One was my view of the 'and/or' concept. I believed that you could have money or love, but not both. A truly wealthy person believes they can have both. This belief of the 'and/or' concept of mine came directly from my upbringing. I believed I could have love *or* money and I chose love. Thus, I lived my life subconsciously sabotaging myself so I would never have money. With my newfound mindset, I made the choice to have money in my life and to keep it.

The second mindset was to stop thinking so much about debt. For much of my adult life the word "debt" consumed me. It was all I thought about day and night. Everything in my life was attached to that. I learned the universal principal of, "What you put attention to grows." Yep, I certainly was growing debt! I would say things like, "I can't afford it," or "I am always in debt". This mindset perpetuated the situation. How many times have you said, "I can't afford that" or, "My clients won't pay that much". There are endless money mindsets that could be holding you back. The trick is that you need to find which ones are holding YOU back and then do the work to address it. No one else can do this work for you.

Patience & Love

In 2015 and 2016 life got hard again. I lost seven people in my family over an 18-month period, many by cancer. The day came when I was sitting by the phone waiting for the call from the doctor to tell me that my stepfather had passed away. Once again, I was filled with grief even though I knew it was for the best. Restlessly, I waited for the call. When the phone did ring, it was the doctor, but not my father's doctor- mine. I did not fully process what she said to me on the phone but I will never forget her soft, gentle and loving voice. She told me that my biopsy was back and I had melanoma, requiring immediate surgery. Two hours after, I received the call that my stepfather had passed. I was completely numb for days. I do not remember much of the next week leading up to my surgery. I could not even tell someone my name. This threw me off my master plan. I am a Type-A personality and was stopped completely in my tracks.

My lesson from this was love and patience. I learned that slow progress is better than fast. Many people like quick fixes and try and get out of debt fast only to end up worse than when they started because their impaired self-worth from their perceived failure. With a healthier self-worth, there will no longer be the need to spend like crazy and fill those voids.

I caution you, do not wait for a major wakeup call to go after what is really important to you in life. I urge you to stop self-sabotaging behaviors that are holding you back or putting you further from your goals and dreams.

In conclusion, looking back I can see that discovering my 'why' and addressing my mindset while practicing patience and love has allowed me to prosper and move from a life of living in debt to a life of freedom and abundance.

And now it's your turn! If you feel like you are craving abundance but do not quite understand how to get it, begin with the three lessons I shared with you today. Take the time to discover your 'why', clean up your money mindset and above all do this with patience and love. The world needs you to fully show up with all your gifts.

I challenge you to take that first step today. You are worth it!

Meet Maria

Maria Conde is a Health, Wealth and Freedom Coach, a speaker and author. Maria is dedicated to empowering women who want to improve their relationship with money, rid themselves of debt and build a new money legacy.

Maria has a 30 year financial leadership background as a professional accountant, as well as many years as a Health, Life and Money Coach. Maria is also the founder of the Love Your Money Podcast.

Maria's personal financial story includes excessive debt and impulsive spending early in life. She has also been at the other end of the spectrum, making significant income both in salary and investments, and not having the mindset or skills to capitalize on this situation. Because of this, many people can relate to her easily. She combines her personal experience and knowledge from her extensive background to bring you life-changing programs and events to improve your money mindset and support you on your journey to living the life you dream of. Maria's passion is to support women to rise to their full potential by giving them the tools to end the self-sabotaging behaviors and mindset that are holding them back from true wealth.

When Maria is not serving her clients she is mom to an amazing daughter, enjoys cooking, gardening, healthy living and food photography. Freedom and true abundance for Maria includes living a life of service and simple, elegant pleasures. She believes everyone has a gift for this world and truly wants all women to have the means to rise emotionally, physically and financially.

Start your journey to true abundance today and join Maria for her podcasts, courses or coaching at www.mariaconde.com.

Chapter 17

When It Ends – You Begin

How to get out of your head and into your body to make positive shifts in your life

"When you get out of your head and into your body, Shift Happens." - Lisa Alentejano Gaetz

I had a great life; a wonderful family, two beautiful boys, a new home, a dog and a good job. With a long time dream of a family trip to Portugal on the horizon, my life seemed blissfully perfect…except it was not. Not at all, and I did not even know it. On the day it all changed, my husband asked me to come into the kitchen, then dropped the seven words that I knew would change my life forever. He said, "I don't want to be married anymore." My mouth went dry; I was unable to speak. I could feel my heart pounding in my chest. I remember a multitude of emotions going through my body, a cold sweat on my skin, anxiety and shock. I had no words, and not a single tear. I just sat there, stunned.

I remember calmly walking from the kitchen to my bedroom, collapsing on the floor, crying uncontrollably. It was an ugly cry, snot and tears running down my face. It felt as though the wind was knocked right out of me. I will never forget those waves of emotions coming at me. I was afraid; I felt helpless. I searched for hope and found none. I was lost, and I was devastated. After a 24-year marriage, and half my life over, what the hell was I to do now? What the hell was he thinking?

It seemed I was about to embark down a path that, sadly, seemed so much more common these days. The national divorce rate is at 48%, and, according to Statistics Canada, marriages typically last for only 13.8 years.

I tried to do everything in my power to figure out how to fix my marriage. I tried counseling, and together we tried seeing a psychologist. I tried to persuade and convince him that his feelings weren't right. I felt helpless and grief stricken. I had never had to deal with grief of losing someone before. The next year was a life-sucking emotional hell. I felt sorry for myself, I felt sorry for my friends, family and kids that had to endure the complete mess I was. I felt abandoned by the one whom I had planned to spend the rest of my life with. My world as I knew it had been ripped apart and had collapsed around me. My title of 'Wife' was poof, gone in a moment notice! It was going to change my life forever.

On reflection, I knew we hadn't always had an easy marriage, even from the start. His family never did accept me. Even from the beginning, they bestowed a very heavy weight upon our new life together by choosing not to attend our wedding. It would be

17 years later when we would have contact with them again. We tried on several occasions to rekindle that relationship with no luck. Having two children, both with an accompanying postpartum depression, created the start of our emotional breakdown. Neither of us knew how to deal with it so we struggled instead.

I was embarrassed for being so dependent, but I was also angry with him for leaving. I switched between begging him to come back and telling him never to come back. I realize now, I was trying to punish him for leaving me. I've come to understand that if he truly wanted to be with me, he never would want to leave in the first place.

To describe this experience, it's like something happening seemingly out of left field. It felt like the green lights all turned red. It was when life said to me, "Not so fast, my pretty! Listen up! You have some homework to do." That homework was ME.

Breakdowns occur when we stray from being true to our core value. In some essential way, we have fallen asleep, and a breakdown is life's way of waking you up.

Can I get a drum roll, please, because this might surprise you; from breakdown comes breakthroughs and what a breakthrough this was for me. When I discovered four months later that he had moved on with another women, something big shifted inside of me. All those emotions I initially experienced came flooding back to me, and drove me to finally stand up for who I was going to be. I became angry. It was like something snapped inside of me. Like putting gasoline in an empty tank, his decision fuelled me. On the day I found out, I made a phone call to him- the dumping ground. Instead of holding back, I welcomed my somewhat-ugly voice that day. Angry, high-pitched, loud, yelling and stinging from all the years of repressed emotions I'd never expressed. I welcomed this new version of myself. She was powerful. Anger overrode fear that day, the one that I would rise up, like the sun on a cloudy day.

I knew I was embarking on a long journey, and along the way I started to see things a little more clearly. My first big "Aha!" moment was realizing that I had become a master 'stuffer' in my marriage. I had stuffed my feelings down and shut my mouth. Along with the 'stuffing', I shut off my voice as well. I was known as the positive upbeat smiley Lisa everybody came to love except ME. On the outside I looked happy, but on the inside, I was crumbling. I became shut down and shut off.

Instead of speaking my truths, I feared them. I cringed at the thought of being judged, criticized or given the silent treatment, as I had experienced in my marriage. These feelings would soon rear their ugly head in new relationships. I started to recognize them as they showed up, and began listening to my body. A tight feeling in my chest and an upset stomach would form when I was uncomfortable, felt vulnerable or challenged. The more I paid attention to what my body was telling me, the more I started to recognize and work through these feelings. I dug deep for courage, and found I was able to create my own boundaries, even when my voice shook.

This newfound behaviour was freeing and necessary for my growth.

I want you to consider this for a moment; do you realize when you hold back from others, you're doing not only a disservice to yourself, but to them as well? Not voicing your opinion is a bit like being the first person to serve yourself at a banquet. You awkwardly sit and wait to eat because you don't want to be the first person to fix a plate, but imagine yourself being that brave soul who is willing to be the first to speak up, and by doing so, allowing others to feel safe for following.

Instead of staying stuck and feeling sorry for myself, I started to show up for myself. It was the kick-yourself-in-the-ass I needed, and it was way overdue. It was about time I started showing up for myself so I could I could show up for others, and boy-oh-boy did I start learning things about myself.

I jumped in with both feet - personal development, reading, journaling, blogging, meditation, yoga, running and just saying yes to experiencing life full out! I even learned how to rock climb and jumped out of an airplane, too. It was a, 'Fight the fear and do it anyways' kind of attitude.

I realized there was a big mess inside my head. I had spent years cluttering it with thoughts of fear, self-defeating messages, doubt, anxiety, worry, resentment, anger and expectations. A mind is a terrible thing to waste. It was time to break up with my mind and make up with my body and spirit.

As time passed, I felt my spirit coming alive, like a seedling newly planted that was gently watered and starting to sprout roots again. With that newfound alive-ness, I decided it was also time to change up my daily workout routine.

I became a Master Chef to my body in many ways. It took some experimenting, but I found the ingredients that I needed to feel right. I made a conscious effort to plan and commit to 'me,' no matter what. I started scheduling me in like that million-dollar client I had always dreamed of. Hot yoga was my newest love and

I attend it four or five times a week- it took me some time to get used to the heat and, quite frankly the sweat and smell, but I was home. It was a place of silence for my mind, body and soul. It was my let-go place of any thoughts or worries for that day. It allowed me to become more centred and present with who I was. It literally changed the way I felt both inside and outside my body. The transformation was incredible. My yoga mat became my best friend. Spin classes and running, the second ingredient. Meditation and journaling was the final, completing my recipe of me. Meditation calmed the mind, and journaling was an outlet to release my thoughts and practice positive affirmations.

Here is what I found; by dropping my excuses, the 'I'm too busy,' I'm too tired,' and all the other BS excuses of why not, the results started to come in. By starting a routine of scheduling it in and committing to that routine no matter what, a habit quickly formed. As we are all creatures of habit, it just kept going. It helped to see results, like real results. I looked and felt amazing and felt accomplished, too. I had more energy for my family, my business and me. It just got easier to commit to it daily, and the best part? My workouts are completed by 7 a.m.

Why then do we continuously take the safe route, make excuses and not do the things we know we should be doing? Well for me, it was fear of failure, lack of motivation or just plain laziness.

But guess what? Not getting started, I realized, was just another type of failure. You end up in the same place, whether you try and fail or whether you don't start at all. The only way to fail is not to try. If you try, you have a chance of succeeding and a chance of failing. If you don't try, you have a 100% chance of failing. Which is the less risky choice?

You may be saying to yourself, "I can't do that early morning thing," or, "I don't have time," or, "I don't have the money." Here's the thing-- we all get 24 hours a day, seven days a week, and it's time to start making yourself a priority. I am all too familiar with putting everybody else first: family, friends and clients. If you don't get yourself right you cannot fully give yourself to others.

This all might hurt, it might be frustrating and you might want to quit or give up, yes. Actually, I can guarantee you that all of the above will at some point apply to each and every one of you. What I always said when I had any type of setback is, "Tomorrow is a new day and I'll pick back up where I left off and get going again." I'm here to tell you it's all a possibility for each and every one of you. If you want to start, JUST START, it's that simple!

Looking back at my journey, I used to think 'poor me', but I realized it was 'for me.' Over a year has passed since my separation, and I have come to realize many things. Our marriage didn't break down just because of him; it broke down because of both of us. The two of us were fools in love and we wanted that fairy-tale wedding and life we dreamed about when we were kids. He was my Prince Charming and I, his princess. We had the house and the kids, but no real direction on how to do it successfully. We made the best of what were given. Sometimes it works, sometimes it doesn't. In our case, it didn't. I don't call it a failure, I call it a long experiment with two good people. We brought two amazing sons into this world that are outstanding human beings, and for that, I am grateful.

It is true when they say, "What doesn't kill you makes you stronger," I can say that for certain. My gift to you is this: don't wait for a major wake up call to start making yourself a priority. At the end of the day, start living and taking care of number one, which is you.

We all have too much to do to sit on the sidelines. I need you to step out of the grey twilight into the bright sunshine and see the dawn of the new day and shine bright. For by doing so, you can give hope to others.

Rise Up Challenge

Forgive Yourself

When I thought there was nothing to forgive myself for, I was wrong. As I went through my process, I needed to let go of many things I had carried throughout my journey. When going through tragedies or hard times, we often hold onto a lot of guilt-- what could I have done better, why didn't I do this sooner, etc. Realize that the past is in the past. There is no point spending time on it anymore. Realize that you did the best you could at the time with what you were given. Forgive yourself, forgive others and remember to be gentle on yourself. Above all, love you.

When You Want to Quit, Do it Anyways

Many times, I found myself here. There were many early mornings I didn't want to get out of bed and work out. Or, I went for the unhealthy burger I knew I shouldn't eat. I didn't drink as much water as I committed to. So what! I'm hear to tell you life happens to all of us. We fall off the wagon often, and it will happen again, I guarantee you. Just don't stop. Get up with the belief that you can and push on. Tomorrow is a new day, as is the next and the next. Just take a step, dig deep and harness that belief in yourself. You can do it!

Get Comfortable with Being Uncomfortable

I learned all too well that being uncomfortable often stopped me from doing many things in my life. A big one was using my voice to express how I feel. Often, it stopped me in my tracks both in business and my personal life, from giving a client bad news or telling my husband how I really felt about something. Take a deep breath and just breathe for a moment, then let it out. Say what you have to say even when your voice shakes or just doesn't feel right. I can tell you this it is so much better than stuffing and holding on to those feelings. The freedom of using your voice is empowering. Try it on, I dare you!

Meet Lisa

Lisa Alentejano Gaetz is an Inspirational Speaker, Author and Mind-Body Connection Coach. She's led a rewarding and successful career in the Financial Industry and with her own business for the past seven years.

When Lisa was faced with a life-changing event, she knew she was destined for something much larger. She used that event to fuel her passion of empowering others to love themselves and inspire change in their own lives by shifting their perspectives on how they connected with their inner and outer being, even during chaos and uncertainty.

Lisa's powerful and inspired message demonstrates how to live an extraordinary and active life that ultimately impacts everything and everyone around you in a positive way. When you show up for yourself and get present with your body, you can fully show up for others. She relates how making simple changes and allowing more time for yourself to stay fit, active and keep moving will help catapult both your business and personal relationships to success.

Her smile is contagious, her energy draws people in and her heart truly inspires those she meets. Her real life, humorous, no BS approach is refreshing and will shift the way you approach your body, your life and your daily routines. She really is the Sparkplug for your "SELF" when your body, mind and spirit are in a real need of a tune up, because she knows and has LIVED her message that when you get out of your head and into your body, "shift" happens. You can find her online at: www.lisagaetz.com.

Chapter 18

A Call To Rise

Face your fears and live your life

"I realized that all along, fear had been showing me the path I was meant to take; it wasn't there to hold me back, but to show me the way." - Chantelle Adams

In our life, we have moments that change us or that guide us to our calling. Though at the time, these moments can feel as if they are breaking us rather than teaching us what we most need to learn. If we can open up to these moments and recognize them for what they truly are- a gift- heeding the call to rise instead of shrink, we will see the lessons and be able to move from the darkness into the light.

This process of transformation creates what I call a "diamond moment," and each of us has one in our lifetime. Sometimes more than one, but we can all likely identify at least one moment where we felt suspended at the edge, ready to break. Then, something finally becomes clear to us, and we know the direction we must go, and realize the change we are called to make and are motivated to change. In each moment we have a choice; a choice to fall back and shrink, or to lean in and trust. As we choose to lean in and believe miracles will unfold, then we will find our path, our purpose and our truth. And when we find our truth, I think it is our duty to share it with the world, because as we shine in our truth and speak up to share our story and message with the world, we give others the permission to do the same.

I remember the moment everything changed for me. I was sitting in the back pew of the church, tears streaming down my face as I mourned the loss of my dear friend. She had lost her fight with breast cancer. Her oldest son, barely out of high school was standing at the pulpit sharing with us his Mom's final hours. He said she was so weak that she was only able to speak in whispers, but he said, "You know, Mom, she was fighting right up to her final breath. She wasn't done fighting because she wasn't done living." As he spoke those words it was as if the wind got knocked out of me, because I realized that although I was sitting there alive and breathing, I was not living my life.

I was shocked by this thought because I had a good life and a good job. I was a mom to three beautiful boys and a wife. We lived in a beautiful home and everything in my life was *fine*. As I heard myself say fine, I realized that yes, I was fine. But fine had become the acceptance of mediocrity. It had come to mean surrendering to what I thought I should be doing and how I thought I should be living. It had come to mean giving up my dreams for the safety of what was within my reach now. I didn't want to live a mediocre existence, and I realized that by being ok with just being ok I was wasting this gift of life.

What I didn't know was WHY I was feeling this way, or how I had unknowingly drifted into a state of just-ok living. When had I forgotten my dreams and who was I? As I dug deep, I discovered that under it all, under every decision I had ever made or not made, was a nasty four-letter word… FEAR!

Fear was what had held me back, kept me playing small, staying safe and fear is what caused me to lose myself and my dreams along the way.

As I reflected back on my life, I saw that almost every single decision I had made was based in fear. Fear of the unknown, fear of rejection, fear of what other's would think, fear of failure, fear of not being good enough, fear of being misunderstood, fear of not being loved in return and the list goes on.

Fear had lead me to this moment of being alive, but not living my life fully. Through this realization, and in my friend's honour I decided to face all my fears. I got out my pen and paper and wrote down 'My Fear List' then proceeded to write everything that I had ever wanted to do but hadn't because I was afraid.

Some of the things on that fear list that I have since conquered are:

- Riding a donkey along a tiny mountain trail, believe me donkeys can run! (fear of running right off the edge of a cliff)

- Rappelling down a waterfall (fear of the ropes breaking)

- Ziplining across amazing rainforests in Puerto Vallarta (fear of heights)

- Hiking Fisher Peak, the tallest peak in the Kootenay's towering over the other peaks at almost 10,000 ft. This is a big feat due to my fear of heights (fear of falling to my death and of course fear of heights)

- Skiing for the first time at age 32 (fear of heights and not being in total control)

- Taking a chance and approaching influential, successful people for collaboration and connection (fear of rejection)

- Starting my own business and seeing it soar! (fear of failure, fear of imperfections)

- Skydiving (fear of plummeting to my death, or breaking both legs, fear of exiting a plane 10,000 ft. above ground...)

- Starting a HUGE fundraising project, The Courage to Fly Project (fear of not raising anything... but we did... we raised $8200... in just three weeks!)

- Asking influential women change-makers to co-author a book, The Courage to Fly (fear of rejection but 60 amazing women came together to write this book including Danielle LaPorte, Nisha Moodley, Karen Salmansohn and many more... and you can get this book for FREE when you sign up for The Courage Revolution!)

- Enter a Latin Dancing Competition (I got to wear a sweet little sequin red dress while dancing the cha-cha and helped raise over $250,000 for charity!)

- Doing a Brave Dance in public! (fear of what others might think)

- Running my first-ever online coaching program, Centre Stage, and helping women entrepreneurs own their story, write their standing-ovation-worthy speech and rock the stage while facing their fear! (fear no one will sign up... but it has sold out EVERY single time!!!)

- Speaking... I faced this one big time delivering over 800 speeches in just five years (fear of rejection and falling flat on my face or forgetting my words)

It is amazing what happens when you write down those big fears you want to overcome. Opportunities begin to appear to help you address your fears and allow you to meet them head on. You Rise.

One of my biggest fears (the first one I wrote down on my fear list) was skydiving, and when I wrote it down, I didn't believe it was going to happen until I got a phone call from a dear friend inviting me to jump out of a perfectly good airplane. Every part of me wanted to say NO, but instead I said, "Heck Yeah, let's do this!" This is something I want to challenge you to start doing... say "HECK YEAH" to the opportunities that come your way- especially the ones that terrify you!

As we set the date and I thought about the moment six weeks down the road when I would be falling 10,000 feet, I began to think of every possible way to get OUT of jumping. Could I fake a serious illness, get called for jury duty, move my whole family to another country?

I realized that for me to jump and face one of my biggest fears, I needed to make my WHY bigger than my fear. I needed to make this about something bigger than me.

I decided in a moment of inspiration to jump out of that airplane and fall 10,000 feet to raise $10,000 to build a school in Nicaragua. This deeper 'why' gave me purpose like nothing I have ever experienced before and I was no longer afraid. I was SO excited because I knew that jumping into my fear would mean education for hundreds of kids and a better future for their families.

Now every time I take a leap of faith I always come back to my WHY and make sure that my 'why' is bigger than any fears that will challenge me to shrink, so I can stand firm and continue taking courageous action.

On that day I remember the storm clouds were rolling in. I climbed into that tiny airplane and gave my family a wave goodbye. The tiny, rickety, plane started climbing higher and higher. I remember feeling the excitement, not fear. I realized that all along fear had been showing me the path I was meant to take; it wasn't there to hold me back, but to show me the way. I changed my perception of fear and saw it as fuel to do the work I was called to do, to show me my next big adventure and to remind me in a very real way that I am not only alive and breathing, but I am also really living! I am living all in and full out, no longer playing it safe or keeping small.

When the door to that tiny plane was opened and the cameraman walked carefully out on the wing of the plane, I knew it was time. I shimmied over to the edge of the plane, swung my feet out of the door and placed them so carefully on the insignificant platform just over the wheel well of the plane. I peered down over my shoes and into the 10,000 feet below me. I realized how high up I was. A wave of fear washed over me, and there was a moment where I wanted to claw my way back into the plane. Instead, I took a deep breath, looked up to the heavens, crossed my hands over my chest, said a silent prayer and then I leaned into that fear and fell.

In that split second of choosing to lean in and fall without having it all figured out, not knowing what was to come after I jumped, I had complete faith and trusted that this was exactly what I was meant to be doing at this moment in time, no matter what the outcome. In the falling, I found my wings, and as I stretched out my arms and fell 5000 feet in 45 seconds. I have never felt more alive or freer. I truly soared that day.

I know that this choice to have courage over fear led me on a journey from one courageous opportunity to another. It has brought me to this place where I have created a multi-six-figure business in just three years. I have traveled the world speaking on almost 1000 stages, co-authored four books with the most incredible women sharing their stories of courage, faced many of my fears and experienced more living in the last five years than I had in my entire life. I have stepped out when I wanted to hide, chosen to speak up when I felt fear begging me to remain silent, launched programs that I knew came to me from a place of divine inspiration. And even though my ego wanted me to play it safe, I went all in without it being perfect, and through imperfect and courageous action, I have created a movement of women's voices being heard around the globe.

With all of this crazy fear busting has come more clarity, confidence and compassion. Facing my fears has given me more courage to swiftly face my existing fears when they appear.

I believe every act of courage leads us to the next moment we are meant to experience. Ultimately, we become exactly who we were always meant to be, and we live life to the fullest with no regrets at the end of our day. We will leave a legacy that inspires many.

I see so many women who are lost, who are unfulfilled, who want more out of life but are too scared to get out there and create what they want, their way. Instead, they settle for the 'I'm fine' life.

I see so many women who let fears keep them chained down and immovable, and this is a place I remember all too well. Trying so hard to please everyone else, to appear perfect, successful and happy when in reality, inside they are crumbling!

I want to help you view who you are with new eyes, to remember and to believe.

I want you to tap into your superpowers and create a life of freedom. No more waiting.

I want to open your eyes to the fact that you are enough; NO, you are more than enough.

I want to help you discover your truth, live with courage and make a big impact in the world because you aren't afraid to step up into your light and shine.

I BELIEVE IN YOU.

I BELIEVE THAT YOU ARE ENOUGH AND I AM READY FOR YOU TO DITCH THOSE FEARS AND UNCOVER YOUR GUIDING TRUTHS.

I believe you are ready to break free from the chains that keep you captive: fear, doubt, envy, shame and reclaim your life.

I believe you are meant to do big things. Own your life and play big, because it is your time to soar!

Now is the time, your life is waiting.

Rise Up Challenge

Write Your Fear List

The first thing I did that started my own personal Courage Revolution was to write down all the things I had ever wanted to do but hadn't, because I was afraid. There was something magical in admitting my desires and my fears, and I do believe when you write things down it opens up the possibilities and opportunities for you to practice getting your brave on.

Take out a sheet of paper and for 15 minutes, don't stop writing. Don't overthink it, just write ALL the things you have ever wanted to do or experience or create from the time you were a little girl but haven't yet because of fear.

I would LOVE for you to share all or some of your list using the hashtag #myfearlist on social media and tag me (Chantelle Adams) so I can cheer you on!

Make your WHY bigger than your fear

I want you to think about your fear list and then choose one BIG fear and think to yourself... what is your big why, the why that is bigger than your fear and bigger than you? If you don't have it yet, make sure you take time to reflect and keep asking WHY until you get to your root 'why'. Your root 'why' will propel you into courageous action and move you through your fear.

I find a 'why' for each big fear I am about to face, so this will be something you come back to over and over.

Say YES to Fear

If you look at your life and see what you have sacrificed or missed out on because of fear and you write your fear list, vowing to live all in and full out, no longer letting fear dictate your choices, opportunities will begin to show up. You will have chances to practice courage, and I challenge you to say HECK YEAH when they do because you will be guided every step of the way, I guarantee it. Say YES to fear and fear will lead you back to YOU and the most incredible life- the one you once only dreamed of living!

Want a little more courage in your life? Check out the Courage Collective: www.thecouragecollective.com.

Meet Chantelle

Chantelle Adams is a Professional Speaker, Speech Stylist and Courage Igniter. She has delivered over 800 speeches and added more than six figures to her business through speaking. Now she teaches women entrepreneurs how to own their story and have the courage to share it while turning their message into a movement!

Chapter 19

This Is Women Rising

"There is no force equal to a woman determined to rise."
- W.E.B. Dubois

Thank you for joining us on this journey of Women Rising. Within these pages, we have had the privilege to learn first hand from the women who have been brave enough to share their experiences with us. We have been invited to share in the most intimate moments of these women's lives. We have learned so much; from the aftermath of a woman's affair and what she learned as she moved towards living a happier life, to the gift in observing a generation that sees things differently than we might see them. And, we have learned about the power of gratitude and how a simple change in thinking can help people move through their most challenging days.

We have heard how a seemingly shameful money story can hold you back, and that abundance is a way you choose to live each day. We have come to understand that your special needs child may be both your teacher and your greatest gift. We have been invited to see how a beautiful thread of magic can be woven into your approach to life, been shown that valuing our worth can set us free and we have heard how embracing your "second birth" can change how you experience life. We have had glimpses at the destructive pull of postpartum depression and been provided with a road to recovery. We have sat with women through their discovery of a diagnosis that would change their lives, and come to see how the elements of nature can play a role in healing and transforming their lives.

We have been asked to consider our self-care practices and to embrace time for ourselves, so we can be better to ourselves and show up in a more powerful way. We have been encouraged to get out of our heads and into our bodies so we can shift from what we have always done to what really works best for us. And, we have been encouraged to face our fears, because fear teaches us what really matters most in our hearts.

And, when we desire more, we have heard how blasting through our comfort zone can put us in a place to receive more of everything we desire. We have been asked to think ahead to a visit from our 90-year-old self and ask ourselves if she would be happy with our choices. And, when we crave different, we have learned that quitting can be okay, because it allows us to experience things in a new way. Finally, we have been asked to think about the legacy we will leave behind in this world.

We have done all of this, and we will continue to do more. To ruminate on all we have learned and carry it forward with us. We will rise, because...

This is Women Rising.

About This Series

The **Women Rising Series** is the brainchild of Chantelle Adams. All three books are available on Amazon. The third in the series is also available for Kindle.

If you enjoy the stories and believe in the importance of Women Rising, please consider leaving a book review on Amazon. Furthermore, should you wish to learn more about the exiting projects Chantelle has on the go, visit her at www.chantelleadams.com. She would love to connect with you!

Made in the USA
Columbia, SC
29 April 2017